Change always begins with conversation. *Meals from Mars* is a conversation starter for those willing to dialogue. Ben Sciacca is a trusted voice filled with the compassion necessary to see gospel-centered change become reality in our social frameworks.

D. A. HORTON
Author of *Bound to Be Free*

Most Americans today are aware of the national divide that is pulling us apart at the seams. However, few are aware of how deep and complex this divide really is. Many choose to attribute it to race, class, or culture, but the issue defies all one-dimensional explanations. *Meals from Mars* brilliantly explores the many facets of this issue as it unfolds the compelling story of how two men and their families navigate these stormy waters. This novel is a useful and necessary tool to help the church begin to rediscover what keeps us from fully functioning as the Body of Christ.

CARL ELLIS JR.
Author of *Free at Last: The Gospel in the African American Experience*

Ben Sciacca has invited us into an important metropolitan tale full of jukes and intrigue. He cleverly weaves the relevant issues of our day with a fast urban plot, which forces thought-provoking self-examination regardless of how you view the matter of lives or lives that matter.

JOHN WELLS
Rap artist The Tonic from The Cross Movement; president/CEO of Cross Movement Records and Issachar Media

Meals from Mars is truly a story America needs to hear. In an entertaining and powerfully engaging way, Ben Sciacca leads us to better understand the challenges of many of the racial tensions facing our nation. Even better, he shows us a glimpse of transformation that can happen in the context of unlikely relationships. I can't wait to give this book to all my friends.

DANNY WUERFFEL
1996 Heisman Trophy winner and executive director of Desire Street Ministries (Atlanta, Georgia)

Meals from Mars is a masterfully compelling narrative that proves helpful in illustrating the difficult nuances of race in America. Sciacca humanizes the struggles of the urban poor and challenges the reader to charitably consider alternative worldviews. *Meals from Mars* invites you to join an American journey, involving the usual suspects, that promises to spark unusually beneficial dialogue.

JASON COOK
Associate pastor of preaching, Fellowship Memphis

Conversations about racial tension are often tough for a number of reasons. It becomes easy to talk past one another when the conversation is reduced to arguments about abstract principles divorced from actual names and faces. *Meals from Mars* doesn't allow that to happen. An eagerness to speak is replaced with silence as you find empathy and sympathy rising up out of nowhere. I couldn't put it down. Such an amazing read. A great primer for getting anyone engaged in this conversation.

JOHN ONWUCHEKWA
Lead pastor, Cornerstone Church, Atlanta

MEALS FROM MARS

A PARABLE OF PREJUDICE & PROVIDENCE

BEN SCIACCA

A NavPress resource published in alliance
with Tyndale House Publishers, Inc.

NAVPRESS

NavPress is the publishing ministry of The Navigators, an international Christian organization and leader in personal spiritual development. NavPress is committed to helping people grow spiritually and enjoy lives of meaning and hope through personal and group resources that are biblically rooted, culturally relevant, and highly practical.

For more information, visit www.NavPress.com.

Meals from Mars: A Parable of Prejudice and Providence

Copyright © 2017 by Ben Sciacca. All rights reserved.

A NavPress resource published in alliance with Tyndale House Publishers, Inc.

NAVPRESS and the NAVPRESS logo are registered trademarks of NavPress, The Navigators, Colorado Springs, CO. *TYNDALE* is a registered trademark of Tyndale House Publishers, Inc. Absence of ® in connection with marks of NavPress or other parties does not indicate an absence of registration of those marks.

The Team:
Don Pape, Publisher
David Zimmerman, Acquisitions Editor
Daniel Farrell, Designer

Cover photograph of businessman copyright © Bulent Ince/Getty Images. All rights reserved.

Cover photograph of man in hoodie copyright © Paul Bradbury/Getty Images. All rights reserved.

Scripture taken from the Holy Bible, *New International Version,*® *NIV.*® Copyright © 1973, 1978, 1984, 2011 by Biblica, Inc.® Used by permission. All rights reserved worldwide.

Some of the anecdotal illustrations in this book are true to life and are included with the permission of the persons involved. All other illustrations are composites of real situations, and any resemblance to people living or dead is purely coincidental.

For information about special discounts for bulk purchases, please contact Tyndale House Publishers at csresponse@tyndale.com or call 800-323-9400.

Cataloging-in-Publication Data is available.

ISBN 978-1-63146-544-4

Printed in the United States of America

23	22	21	20	19	18	17
7	6	5	4	3	2	1

For my beloved wife, Sara. I'm so grateful for you and your fierce love for me, our family, and our city.

(Jeremiah 29:7)

CONTENTS

THE END

1:12 p.m., Tuesday before Thanksgiving

"STEP OUT OF THE VEHICLE WITH YOUR HANDS IN THE AIR!"
Clouds of steam billowed from under the crumpled hood of the Lexus. Glass from the driver-side rear window lay strewn along the road, sparkling like diamonds on the glistening blacktop. Two police SUVs encircled the wreckage, their lights ricocheting around the snow-laden trees that hugged the edges of the road.

Jim slowly lifted his aching head and squinted through the window at the scene outside the car. Through the iced front windshield he could see the shadowy silhouettes of three officers with drawn pistols. They shielded themselves behind their open car doors. A thick hot strand of blood meandered slowly down Jim's face from a ragged cut above his left eye. His head throbbed.

One of the police officers was bellowing something, but Jim couldn't make out the words. He slowly rolled his eyes over to the driver seat to see if Malik was okay.

Malik was alert, wide-eyed, as the red and blue lights refracted onto his face like a kaleidoscope. His hair was littered with broken glass. Clouds of breath emerged from his open mouth in the frozen air. An abrasion on the side of his face was spotted with blood. Probably the airbag. He glanced for a moment at Jim out of the corner of his eye before leaning forward and fumbling around the brake pedal.

"Come on, Malik," Jim said with a hoarse whisper. "It's all over now, son."

Malik ignored Jim. His eyes flashed as his hand found what he was looking for. As he pulled the black handgun from the floorboards, he groaned.

Jim looked at the gun, now resting in the young man's lap, and then at Malik. "Think, son," Jim said, placing his hand on the young man's shoulder. "This is not a good idea. It's over."

Malik frowned as he stared out the window.

"Get out of the vehicle with your hands in the air. Now!" the officer hollered again.

"You're right, Jim," Malik said in a near whisper. "It *is* all over—for me at least."

Jim swallowed and shot a nervous look at the police cars. Malik continued to stare out the front window with a grim face.

"Just give me the gun, Malik," Jim said. He placed his open hand in front of Malik's chest. "Those men outside will kill you if you step out with that."

Malik exhaled a deep sigh but said nothing.

"Give me the gun, Malik, and we both walk out of here alive today."

Malik took a long look at the gun in his hand. He shook his head. "Man, too much has happened. Too much. I'm dead no matter what." A slight smile emerged at the corner of his lips as a lone tear fell from his eye. He stuffed the gun into the front waistband of his pants. The handle was barely visible. He pressed the button to unlock his door.

Jim grasped frantically for Malik's shirt, but the young man opened the door and stepped out of the car into the frigid air before he could catch him.

THE SAMARITAN

Twenty hours earlier

MARY BETH FROWNED. Her face was taut as she applied eye shadow with quick deliberate strokes. "I don't know why it has to be you, Jim. And tonight? Why tonight?"

Jim sighed and leaned on the door frame of their bedroom as his wife continued to put on her face in the bathroom. She was thin, pretty. She wore a bright red dress, and her dark black hair was pulled into a braid that rested between her bare shoulders. At age thirty-four she looked surprisingly young, but her slightly strained expression always suggested it was requiring great concentration to hold all the facets of her face together.

"I didn't think our turn would ever come," he said with a sigh. "You and I are way down the list, and, well, I just figured we were safe to avoid actually having to do something like this."

"We?" Mary Beth said with a slight sneer. "I'm not going down there. It's almost five o'clock. And you're not going down there either, Jim. I'm sure it can wait till morning."

Jim shook his head. "No it can't. These folks have already been waiting for a week. They're hungry, honey. Besides, it's Thanksgiving in three days and we're heading out of town. I don't want to do it, but—"

"Then don't," his wife said plainly. "I'm sure Pat and Sally can go. Don't they usually do this errand?"

"They do, but they're traveling to see Pat's family."

"What about Ed? He's single. I'm sure he's free tonight."

"He's in Italy."

Mary Beth exhaled an exasperated sigh. "Well isn't that convenient? Did no one think about this before they skipped town?"

"Look. I've given this tons of thought. There's seriously no one else, baby. I'm sorry." Jim rounded the corner and stepped into the bathroom where Mary Beth was leaning into the mirror and applying some lipstick. "The trunk is already full of groceries. If I get going, I bet I can be back by seven."

"It'll be dark. I don't like that. Besides, seven is pushing it. My parents are coming at eight. Isn't that reason enough to wait?" She looked hopefully at Jim's reflection in the mirror.

"We've been discussing this whole thing on and off for the last two hours. I need to go. There are refrigerated things in my trunk. I have the address. If all goes well, I'll be back with plenty of time to help you get set up for your parents tonight. But I need to go. Now."

Mary Beth shot a glance at her husband and frowned again. She shook her head slightly.

"Always the do-gooder, aren't you? I don't think this family—whoever they are—would starve if they got these groceries tomorrow. You have no idea how the thought of you going down into that neighborhood at night makes me worry. This really frustrates me."

Jim jostled the car keys in his pocket. "I'm nervous too, hon. But I'm going. Don't even worry about this. I don't want you to stress out our little girl there." He smiled as he stole a glance at the tiny bump in his wife's belly.

Jim and Mary Beth had been married for four years, but neither of them had wanted children until Jim's law practice took off. Both sets of parents had told them that having kids before establishing financial stability would be a mistake. But Jim's career had taken off, and they were able to buy the house in Stone Brook that they wanted. It was only practical to start trying for kids. Mary Beth was six months along with their firstborn, a girl. They planned to call her Katelyn.

Jim took another step into the bathroom and placed his hands on his wife's shoulders. The two stared at each other in the mirror. He lowered his hands slowly down her sides and then gently placed his arms around her stomach. She smiled just slightly.

"I'll be home at seven, dear," Jim said before placing a soft kiss on her neck.

She flinched slightly. "That tickles."

"You look beautiful tonight."

"Hurry home, Jim," she said, placing her hands on his. "And bring a coat. It's supposed to drop below freezing tonight."

"You got it!" Jim said. He snagged his North Face fleece off the coat rack in the corner of the room. "You need anything at all, just call me. Okay?"

"Okay, honey. See you soon. Please be careful—are you going to bring your gun?"

Jim laughed. "What? My hunting rifle? Come on, dear. I don't think so."

"My dad used to bring a gun when he drove to that side of town. And I know for a fact that Daddy was never down there when it was dark."

"Honey, I'm dropping off a turkey—not hunting for one. I'll be fine." Jim's voice betrayed a slight hint of annoyance. "Goodbye. I love you."

With that Jim spun on his heels and headed down the stairs to the garage. Mary Beth sat down on the bed and played with her large diamond wedding ring, rolling it with her thumb while she stared at the floor. She heard the garage door open beneath her. With slow steps she walked to the bedroom window and gently pulled back one of the curtains just in time to see Jim's black Lexus move down the driveway, onto the street, and out of sight.

3

THE ERRAND

5:30 p.m., Monday before Thanksgiving

MALIK RUBBED HIS HANDS TOGETHER, placed them over his mouth, and blew two sharp breaths before stuffing them into the goose-down pockets of his black jacket. He glanced at the thermostat on the wall. Forty-seven degrees. He pulled his stocking cap over his ears and grimaced. A book of world history was open in his lap.

Malik was a tall and lanky kid. Lighter-skinned than his brother and sisters, he had kind brown eyes and a shy smile. He was working on a mustache, and a tuft of black hair protruded from his chin. At eighteen years of age he was unusually quiet and kept mostly to himself. Most of his conversations took place via text messages on his phone.

"Malik!"

He looked up from his book. "Yeah, Grandma. I'm comin'."

His grandmother's apartment was small and plain. The living room had two old brown couches with tufts of stuffing that erupted from the cushions here and there in little geysers. Her carpet was stained and weatherworn from years of traffic. The walls were papered with a violet floral pattern. Pictures of Malik's mother and her sister and brother hung on the wall. An old television sat atop a wooden end table in the corner of the living room. There were cartoons playing, and his younger brother and sisters sat on the floor, watching the show as they devoured handfuls of popcorn from a large orange bowl.

Malik wandered into the kitchen. His grandmother smiled at him, her eyes twinkling with joy. Her aged hands and the blue apron she was wearing were covered with flour. Malik was always amazed by the miraculous meals his grandmother created in such a tiny space. With just the two of them standing in the kitchen together, it felt crowded.

"Baby," she said softly, "I'm so sorry, but I'm gonna need you to run to the store."

"Okay. What'cha need?"

"If I'm gonna make those biscuits you like, then I'm gonna need some more butter and milk." She shook her head. "I thought we'd have what we needed."

"It's no problem," he said with a grin of his own. "I can go. That all you need?"

"I think so, baby. Now let me get you some money." She left the kitchen and headed toward her bedroom.

Malik's cell phone chirped. He pulled it out of his pocket to check a text message from his friend Brenden.

Shots poppin' on 44th. Them field Boyz aint playin.

Malik frowned and glanced out the window as he put his phone back in his pocket. The apartments behind them were silhouetted in a wall of orange and purple fire—the sun was almost gone for the day. He mumbled something under his breath and walked into the bedroom he shared with his brother Jamal. Looking over his shoulder to see if his grandmother or one of his little siblings was nearby, he opened his closet. Stretching up high on his tiptoes, he felt around under a pile of sweatshirts on his top shelf until he found what he was looking for. He took one more look toward the door—Jamal was nosey and often appeared out of nowhere—before pulling down a black handgun. He stuffed it quickly in the back of his pants.

"Malik!" His grandmother hollered again. "Where'd you go, son?"

"I'm here. Just one sec."

He reappeared in the living room to find his grandmother leafing through her billfold. She handed him a ten-dollar bill. "That should cover things. If there's anything left over, grab yourself a candy bar or something."

Malik resented the fact that his grandmother had to live like this. She worked as a custodian for a big white church on the other side of town. His mom hadn't been home for two months; she had gone to live with her boyfriend a few blocks down the street after his grandmother had put her out for stealing again. Now she was housing Malik and the other three kids until his mom got her life together. They'd been living there for the last six months. Putting food on the table had strained her so much that she was two months behind on the heat bill. This last week they were feeling the harsh cold after the temperatures had plummeted into the low thirties.

"Be safe, Malik," his grandmother said, placing a hand on his face. "It's cold and dark out there. Keep your eyes open and—"

"And mind your surroundings," Malik said with a grin. "I know. I'll be careful. You know I will." He stuffed his grandmother's money up under his stocking cap. "Thank you, Grandma—for everything . . . You think mom will come on Thursday?"

Malik's grandmother sighed. "I got no idea what your mother's gonna do, Malik. She's welcome to come for some food if she wants. If there's any meal that brings family together, it's Thanksgiving."

Malik's lips tightened, and he nodded slightly. "Aight. Well, I'll be back in a minute."

"Okay hon. Be safe."

Malik walked slowly down the stairs and exited the apartment. The screened door swung shut behind him with a bang. He winced as the cold evening air stung his face. The streetlights buzzed and started to flicker on, like lightning bugs roused from a deep sleep. The temperature had forced almost everyone inside. Tendrils of smoke curled slowly from a few chimneys. The smell of burning wood met his nostrils. He loved that smell.

Malik hoisted his pants and tightened his belt. The

gun in his back waistband gave him a sense of assurance as he started walking down the sidewalk toward the small convenience store at the end of the street. The cold and the darkness were antagonists he neither liked nor welcomed. The store was four blocks away, but on a night like this, it felt more like four miles to him. He hunched his shoulders slightly but held his head high.

4

THE DELIVERY

5:37 p.m., Monday before Thanksgiving

JIM GRIPPED HIS STEERING WHEEL with both hands as he drove down I-39. He glanced at the clock on his dashboard: 5:37. He hadn't been to the other side of town more than a few times as a kid. His dad had grown up there, but like a lot of white folks, his dad's family moved out once the neighborhood started to change.

Jim's grandfather had been a manager at the steel plant back when business was booming. His dad used to talk about the "good ole days" when Edgewood was a proud community. Now his dad spoke of the place with disdain, shaking his head about the crime. "The community has gone to the dogs," he'd say. Jim's dad wouldn't approve of this errand he was running.

In fact, none of his friends or family would. Jim recalled

playing a basketball game against one of the schools in the area when he was in high school. None of the fans from his school made the trip. He still remembers his dad leaning into the bus and lecturing the coach before they left for the game. "Make sure these boys come home immediately after the game ends!" Most of Jim's friends spoke of Edgewood in the same way they spoke about third-world countries. Edgewood, to them, was "dirty," "unsafe," "poor." The evening news offered a similar message, with regular stories on crime, house fires, and violence.

Jim's trunk was loaded up with two boxes of groceries. His Sunday school class had "adopted" the custodian at their church, Wilma Thompson. Jim, like most people in his class, had never met her or even seen her before, but those who knew her there said she was a wonderful old lady. News had circulated that she was going through some hard times, and the story of her taking in her four grand-kids was compelling. So the class began collecting a weekly ration of groceries for her. Wilma rode the bus to work, so she couldn't carry the groceries home with her from work. The class had to bring them to her.

This little ministry had gone on for almost two months now. Pat and Sally, the couple who had started it, even created a Facebook fan page—"Westside Hope"—where they posted pictures of themselves delivering food to Wilma and her grandchildren. The page had more than two hundred likes, and friends and church folk gave the Sunday school class consistent kudos for the small operation.

Pat and Sally were in their late thirties. They couldn't have kids, so they had a lot of time on their hands—at least that's what Jim and Mary Beth told each other. Members of the Sunday school class faithfully brought canned goods or contributed some cash each Sunday, but few volunteered to drive the groceries to Edgewood. Jim finally signed himself and Mary Beth up as backups to the backup. He never figured he'd actually have to make the trip. If it weren't the Thanksgiving holidays he probably would have waited for another time, but his conscience wouldn't let him.

Jim drove down I-39 and noted the change in landscape as he rounded the downtown and headed toward the west side. The hard brick buildings loomed along the road like monsters. The trees beside the interstate were naked and brown, standing like skeletons against the fiery backdrop of the sunset along the horizon. To his right he noted a tall mountain of gravel and the yawning vast hole beneath it. His GPS alerted him that his exit was just a little over a mile ahead.

As he drew closer to Edgewood, the houses along the interstate became smaller and more tightly clustered. They appeared to be tucked into the hill like hobbit holes, where dim orange lights shown behind drawn curtains.

Just then a flash on his dashboard caught his eye.

"You've got to be kidding me!" Jim shouted. His gas light had come on.

Jim's car was only two years old, but he had learned from experience that when that light came on, he had only ten to fifteen miles before he'd be completely out of fuel. He pressed the button on his dash: 4.7 miles left until empty. The light must have been on longer than he thought.

"Stupid!" he said through gritted teeth. "Where am I going to get gas down here?"

Jim's GPS notified him that his exit was just ahead. He threw on his blinker and merged down the exit ramp. The light at the end of the exit was red, and he had to wait for passing vehicles before he could take his turn onto the street. He looked out the window and noticed that the curb along the edge of the street was littered with cans, bottles, and bags. Beyond the curb was an abandoned field with random patches of dead grass. Three small children were walking through the center of it with plastic sacks in their hands. On the corner, just eight feet from his vehicle, a man sat against a pole in the ground. "Help. I need food," read the cardboard sign in his hands. His face was hidden behind a gnarly beard, and his clothes were dirty.

Suddenly, the two men made eye contact. Jim slowly raised his hand and depressed the door lock.

Directly in front of Jim was a strip of stores. He noticed a nail salon, a tattoo parlor and a Seafood Express restaurant. Farther down the road he spied three gas stations. He checked the GPS: 1.8 miles to Wilma's. He'd have to fill up somewhere along this road if he wanted to get home.

The way finally cleared for Jim to take his right-hand turn. He drove slowly into Edgewood. Under the dim streetlights he could see the houses. They were surprisingly small—old shotgun houses from the steel days. Many of them had bars on the windows. A few were boarded shut.

A dark-gray Cadillac passed Jim on the left, blaring bass that caused Jim's rearview mirror to vibrate. He swallowed nervously and took another look at the light on his dash. Another turn was coming, just a mile up the road.

Jim was bothered by his nervousness. He wasn't used to feeling like this. As a lawyer defending big-name companies from criminal charges, he was familiar with high-pressure situations. But when was the last time he had felt this afraid? How could delivering groceries in Edgewood be scarier than speaking in a courtroom full of angry millionaires?

A few light drops of moisture started to stick on his windshield. Jim instinctively threw on his wipers. They squealed and dragged the drops across the glass in long streaks.

"I hope Wilma is home," he said glumly. "Wouldn't that be my luck . . ."

GPS told him to take a right. Directly across the street from his turn was a brightly lit Shop n' Snack. A few young men were loitering on the sidewalk outside. They turned their heads and watched him as he made his turn. The street, 42nd, was unusually dark—the streetlights softened the night only slightly.

Cars were parked on either side of the road, so Jim proceeded slowly. He craned his neck forward, looking for 917. A young man in a black jacket shuffled along the sidewalk in the opposite direction. "Come on. Come on," Jim hissed through clenched teeth. "Where are you, Eastbrook?"

. . .

He was nearing the end of the road when his navigation
system announced, "You have arrived at your destination."
To his left was the Eastbrook apartment complex. The
nearest streetlamp was partially shielded by the limbs of a
large oak tree. Many of the windows were boarded over with
plywood. The paint on the outside was an olive green, but it
was peeling and torn as if shredded by the claws of a massive
animal. The chain-link fence was broken in various places,
with a thin layer of paper and trash trapped and accumu-
lated at its base.

Jim squinted and tried to find 917 somewhere on one of
the buildings, but it was too dark. He swallowed. He had
come this far. Now it was time to complete his mission.

He popped his trunk and stepped out of the car. Needles
of cold pricked his face and hands. A screen door banged
loudly to his right, causing him to jump. An older fat man
stepped out onto his patio, a sack of garbage in his hand.
He stared at Jim for a moment, then stepped into the yard
and tossed the bag onto a garbage heap on the other side
of the fence. Jim watched as the man ambled back into
his apartment.

Jim stacked the boxes of groceries on top of one another
and hoisted them out of the trunk with a grunt. He
attempted to close his trunk with his elbow, but the trunk
snapped back up. He tried again; this time the trunk stayed
closed. He placed the groceries on the back of his car and

pressed the "lock" button on his key. His car lights flashed twice; the isolated chirp of his car alarm ricocheted down the block.

Jim kept his eyes on the pavement as he moved briskly across the street and into the yard. The front door to the apartment complex was old and rusted. He secured the boxes under his chin and leaned forward to open the door before lurching awkwardly to the side as it opened swiftly on its own. A massive Hispanic kid walked through. He looked Jim up and down for a moment while talking on his cell phone, then glanced over Jim's shoulder at his Lexus.

"What's up?" the kid asked.

"Uh, I'm here to drop off some groceries for Wilma Thompson." Jim felt awkward. "You know where she lives?"

The kid studied Jim for a moment, and then mumbled slowly, "Yeah. She's on the third floor. Room G."

Jim lowered his head and moved out of the way so the kid could pass by. The teenager brushed by him and out into the yard, chuckling something into his phone about a "crazy white dude."

Jim had to adjust his eyes to the dimly lit hallway as he entered the apartment building. A small sign in the middle of the hall pointed to the stairs. He plodded slowly to the stairwell and began to go up. As Jim neared the second floor, his face soured. A pungent odor filled his nostrils. He exhaled loudly. Down the hall, a baby was screaming, and a mother was shouting at her children. The stairs were sticky. Jim tried to guide his leather shoes to a clean spot on each step. From down below him he heard someone yelling in Spanish. He quickened his pace.

The boxes of groceries were cumbersome, and Jim longed to find apartment 3G. He fantasized about simply ringing the doorbell and leaving the groceries at the front door. Finally he reached the third floor and rounded the corner. The hall was dark, aside from two small lightbulbs at each end. Directly in front of him was 3D. He shuffled down the hall until he spotted 3G on his left.

The G on the sign was dangling conspicuously on a peeling and scarred white door. Jim twisted his body with some effort and managed to rap his knuckles on the door. He waited for a moment. No answer. He was stooping to lower the groceries to the floor when he heard soft footsteps approach. Fingers on the other side of the door were fumbling with the locks and latches. Then the door was pulled back slightly, and two eyes peered out at him curiously.

"Uh, hello," Jim said softly. "I'm Jim. I'm here to bring some food to Wilma Thompson. Is she here?"

The set of eyes continued to stare up at him. Jim tried a smile. "Is Wilma here?" He was getting impatient.

The door opened further revealing the small, brown face of a little girl in a long, pink dress. Her hair was pulled back in a ponytail. She looked like she was ten or eleven years old. From behind her appeared another little face, forcing its way under her arm and out into the hallway. The small girl finally managed to squeeze past the first girl and offered Jim a wide grin. She was missing several teeth, but her eyes were beaming with life. Two little trails of crusted snot ran from her nose to her lips.

Jim offered the little girl an awkward grin and cleared his throat. The older girl turned her head over her shoulder and hollered. "Grandma! There's a man here!"

From somewhere back in the apartment Jim heard slow and deliberate steps. The two children parted ways as Wilma emerged and opened the door. Her face was kind, and as she smiled a furrow of wrinkles rippled around her eyes and the corners of her mouth. She was dressed in a light sweater.

"I'm so sorry, hon," she said as she sighed. "My granddaughter doesn't know her manners. Are you from the church?"

"Yes . . . I brought you guys some groceries . . . for Thanksgiving."

Wilma smiled again. "Oh wonderful! I don't think we've met. I'm Wilma Thompson."

"I'm Jim," he replied. "Jim Dawkins." He shifted his weight to manage the load in his arms.

Wilma stepped to the side and placed a callused hand on his. "Please come on in, Jim."

Jim hated the strong urge he had to shake free from her grip, drop the food on the floor, and run down the stairs. He hated even more the color he could feel flushing around his neck and his ears. It emerged whenever he was nervous or embarrassed. Reluctantly he followed Wilma down the short hallway.

He couldn't believe how cold it was inside. The pictures on the wall jumped out at him: A young man wearing military clothing. A smiling young man in a white tuxedo, standing next to a young woman in a short purple dress. It looked like a prom picture. The last frame featured a young lady in a graduation gown.

It didn't take long to reach the living room, where the two girls who met Jim at the door had returned to watching cartoons on a small television. A little boy sat with them. Every few seconds the screen would jolt into static. The volume was too loud. Jim noted the sagging brown couches and, just above them, a painting of a black Jesus.

On the other side of the couches was a shiny brown table with six chairs. Jim turned his head and spotted a tiny restroom and two bedrooms. The apartment was very clean, but there was a slight smell of mildew. And so cold!

Jim rounded the corner into the kitchen, where he nearly collided with Wilma, who was waiting on him. An old refrigerator buzzed behind her in the corner. A tiny pantry space was situated just above a white stove. On the opposite side of the kitchen was a small sink; next to it was some counter space with a large metal bowl full of dough on it.

"Please set those down here, hon." Wilma pointed to the space beside the stove. Jim lowered the groceries. In the cramped space his movement felt slow and exaggerated.

"Could I get you some coffee, Jim?" Wilma asked. "It's freezing outside, isn't it?"

"Uh, no, no," Jim mumbled. He whipped his wrist up in

a quick motion and shot an imaginary glance at his watch. "I need to be going soon."

Wilma had begun rummaging through the first box. Slowly she surveyed the items before turning to the pantry. It was barren, Jim noticed, aside from two cans of chicken soup and a package of ramen noodles. A pleasant grin emerged on Wilma's face as she replenished the empty cupboard with canned beans, corn, and some boxes of instant mashed potatoes and stuffing. A small freezer bag contained broccoli, cauliflower, and celery.

"Do you need any help?" Jim asked as he stood there. He regretted asking such a stupid question the minute the words left his mouth.

"No, sweetheart. Thank you," Wilma said. She emptied the top box and moved on to the second one. In another freezer bag she discovered a turkey.

"Oh! Thank you," she exclaimed. "This is wonderful."

Some items Wilma placed in an otherwise empty fridge; others she added to the pantry. Toward the very bottom of the box was a small tub of hummus and a box of crackers. A curious twinkle emerged in her eyes as she put them in their proper place.

Finally she was done. She turned to face Jim and placed her warm hand on his.

"Jim, this is really a blessing. Lord knows I prayed that we'd have something to eat for Thanksgiving." She lowered her voice slightly. "But honestly, around five o'clock I started losing hope on it. The church has been good to us. My grandbabies and me appreciate the help. I wish my oldest grandson, Malik, was here to meet you, but he's gone to the store for me."

"It's not a big deal," Jim said, taking a slight step backward. "I wish we could have done more."

"Before you go, let me introduce you to my babies." She called to her grandchildren as she moved toward the living room. "Y'all come here and say 'thank you' to Mr. Dawkins."

The three kids got up from the floor and shuffled slowly over to where Jim was standing. The oldest held her head down and looked slightly annoyed. Wilma put her arm around her and pulled her close. "This is Monique," Wilma said proudly. "She's eleven and she looooves basketball, don't you, baby?"

Monique offered a quick half-smile and nodded slightly.

Wilma placed her hand on the other little girl's head. "This little toothless thing is Janae. And Janae loves her some candy." Wilma chuckled as Janae let out a snorting laugh and nestled her head into her grandmother's leg.

"Then finally, there's our little man, Jamal." Wilma said this with a fake frown. "Jamal stays busy. Little man won't sit still for nothin'."

"It's nice to meet all of you," Jim said. "I'm Jim Dawkins . . . Your grandmother works at our church . . . I brought some food for Thanksgiving—" He abruptly stopped speaking to stop the nervous words from gushing out of his mouth.

"Well, Mr. Jim needs to get going. You babies tell him

thank you for the food and for stopping by to see us," Wilma said.

"Thank you Mr. Jim!" the two little ones said in unison. Monique just sucked her lips in and stared at the floor.

The closure Jim was finally sensing was invigorating. He backpedaled quickly down the hallway. "I hope you have a wonderful Thanksgiving! Enjoy the food! Thank you for letting me visit with you! I hope to see you again!" Jim was almost shouting over his shoulder as he walked towards the door. He reached for the handle but stopped as Jamal wrapped his arms around his leg. For a second he froze. Jamal continued to hug him, his chubby face smiling up at him. Jim tentatively patted the boy's head, like he was testing a stove to see if it was hot.

"Okay," Jim chuckled. "Thanks for the hug there, buddy . . . I gotta go now . . ."

Jamal continued to hold on. Jim glanced at Wilma. He could feel his neck and ears flushing again. He laughed nervously.

"C'mon baby," Wilma chided the boy and gently grabbed his arm. "Time to let Mr. Jim go home."

Jamal released his grip and walked slowly back to his grandmother. Jim pulled the door open and gave the Thompson family one more quick look. "Nice to meet you," he said with a wave of his hand. "Good night."

Wilma, Jamal, and Janae were waving at him as he shut the door. With swift and deliberate steps he moved toward the stairwell. He kept his eyes on the ground and descended with the vigor of a man fleeing for freedom. Out of the corner of his eye he saw the silhouette of two figures just beyond the stairs. He heard some angry voices from the end of a hallway. Finally he made it to the bottom and shot straight out of the front door.

The frozen night wind slashed at him the moment he emerged, but he inhaled the frigid air gladly, like a drowning man bursting up from the depths. He whipped his keys from his pocket and clicked the toggle as he rushed across the yard to his car. Jim threw open the door, sat down, and fired up the engine. His heart swelled, a cocktail of relief and shame, with an unusual sense of heroism. Then he cursed. The ominous yellow light reappeared on his dash. The groceries were done, but he still had to get gas. The night wasn't over.

THE DETECTIVE

5:45 p.m., Monday before Thanksgiving

MARQUAN COLE PUT HIS CAR IN PARK AND FROWNED. He looked out of the window as a sharp breeze tossed leaves across the street. The house to his right was more like a castle. The ornate stonework was immaculate. A warm orange light shone behind curtains in more windows than he could count. An elderly white woman, bundled under a thick brown afghan, stood angrily jabbing her finger at one of the two officers in her yard.

MarQuan inhaled a deep breath and exhaled it slowly. He rubbed his hands in front of the dash heater. He needed a moment to brace himself for the cold—and for the ire that Ms. Tessly was about to unload on him.

He opened his door and shrugged his way through the wind. Ms. Tessly's shrill voice clawed its way into his ears like a parasite. He glanced at the two officers, standing just beneath her front patio. They were frozen like snowmen. Their faces were pink and flushed. They'd been standing there for a while.

"Ms. Tessly!" MarQuan bellowed loudly as he walked briskly up the long, bricked driveway.

The old woman pulled the hand she'd been waving wildly in the air back into her blanket for warmth. She shot her eyes over to MarQuan and grimaced. "It happened again, MarQuan!"

MarQuan smiled. "What happened, Ms. Tessly?"

"Some hooligans stole another package off of my patio! This is the third time, MarQuan—the third time!"

Officer Parks cleared his throat. "Detective Cole, we were just talking to Ms. Tessly about getting a description of the 'hooligans.'"

"Did you see them, Ms. Tessly?" MarQuan pulled a notebook from his overcoat.

The old lady snarled. "I didn't see them take my package, but I've definitely seen *them*."

MarQuan clicked his pen and raised his eyebrow, urging her to continue.

"It's that same group of black boys! We've been over this before. They wander around in the community—up and down the streets. Wearing their hoodies with their britches hanging off their butts. They're like ghosts! As soon as I go to grab my phone, poof! They vanish! But they're the ones—it's either them or one of those Mexican construction crews. This isn't rocket science stuff, gentlemen!"

MarQuan made a few pecks on his notebook. "Have you seen any of these people doing anything suspicious— seen them running off with someone else's package, casing anyone's property?"

Ms. Tessly groaned and shook her head. "No I haven't, but that doesn't matter, does it? Do those kids live over here? Do they work over here? I'm not a detective like you, but I'm pretty sure I can spot something suspicious. Besides, I'm not the only one. The Sandersons, Petersons, and Kirklands have also had some UPS packages disappearing off of their porches. With Christmas around the corner, this is only going to get worse. We shouldn't have to worry about stuff disappearing out of our yards, should we?"

Officer Rudolph shifted his weight and spoke slowly. "She's got a point, detective. What are those kids doing way over here?"

"I told her we've been patrolling around since her last call," Officer Parks mumbled, "looking for black—looking for youth that look like they aren't up to any good. We just haven't seen anything yet."

Ms. Tessly ignored Officer Parks and directed her focus on the detective. "I'm running out of patience, MarQuan, and I'm starting to wonder if you really care about this problem. People in Stone Brook are here in this community so that this type of stuff doesn't happen. I have nothing against you personally, but I'm one incident away from filing an official complaint with your supervisor."

She kept going, looking at MarQuan but talking to no one in particular. "No one should have to worry that their Amazon order is going to walk off their porch in the hands of some thieving thugs. At the next neighborhood meeting, I'm going to petition once again to get that bus stop moved another three blocks away. There's no need to have a bus stop so close to Stone Brook. No one from here rides the bus anyway. Maybe the maids will have to walk a few more feet, but that might keep those kids from bothering our neighborhood. Either that or I'm going to need to pay for a gate at the end of my driveway—and that's expensive!" She huffed in frustration. "I feel like no one is listening to me anywhere. It's time to get something done about this!"

MarQuan looked at the ground for a moment before raising his eyes with the slightest smile. "I'm sorry about your packages, Ms. Tessly. I know that's frustrating. If this is a trend, we'll catch whoever is doing these things—I'm sure of that."

Ms. Tessly offered a weak smile of her own. "I know that as a black man you've got to be tired of seeing all of these poor black kids getting arrested. I understand that—we all do. But wrong is wrong. This needs to stop. You told me you'd do something last time we spoke, and here we are again. So let's do something about it."

The detective sucked in his lips and stared at the old woman. The old lady matched his tense gaze for a moment but then looked away and shuddered in the cold. She spun on her heels and grabbed the doorknob to her home. The yard was bathed in light as she threw open the door.

"A cold night like this one would have been a great night for some mint tea," she mumbled absently as she stepped back into her house. "Too bad my tea never made it."

With that she closed the door, leaving MarQuan and the two officers in the cold darkness.

6

THE DRAMA

5:50 p.m., Monday before Thanksgiving

"AYE, MALIK!"

Habib, the store manager, waved at the young man. Bells clanged as the door opened and shut.

Malik nodded a hello. He was grateful to be inside where it was warm. He had been coming to this Shop 'n' Snack since he was a little boy. The three aisles were familiar—staples in his life. He was only eighteen, but he had lived in thirteen different places. This convenience store was a consistent anchor for him. The smell of the hot dogs turning on the rotisserie, even the faint but sweet odor of the cigarettes Habib smoked in his back office, were things he enjoyed.

Habib was old and balding. He had a silvery mustache and a thin gold necklace. He had been running this small convenience store for as long as Malik could remember. Ordinarily he was at his cash register, secured behind bulletproof glass. At the moment, however, he was on his knees, unloading a box of motor oil onto a shelf. Some smooth jazz was playing on the radio. He hummed along absentmindedly as Malik walked over to the refrigerated section.

"Man, why are you out in this cold, boy?" Habib hollered over the aisles. "It's freezing out there!"

"Grandma—she needs some butter and milk." Malik yanked the refrigerator door open and grabbed a gallon of 2 percent.

"How's Ms. Wilma doing?" Habib queried. "I haven't seen her in some time."

"She's aight."

Malik moved to his left and grabbed a box of butter. He looked over his shoulder as some car lights flashed through the store window. A black Lexus pulled into the parking lot and stopped at one of the pumps. Meanwhile, three figures in hoodies were shuffling down the sidewalk, moving toward the store. Clouds of breath emerged from their hoods, but Malik couldn't see their faces.

■ ■ ■

Jim pulled up to the pump. He was grateful there were no other cars in the lot. His completion of this mission couldn't happen any sooner. The idea of a hot meal with his wife and her parents filled him with warmth. He grabbed the car door and opened it slowly, wincing as a thin sheet of sleet stung his face.

"I hope these pumps take credit cards," he muttered.

To his relief, they did. He swiped his Visa and began to fill his tank. The numbers on the pump rolled slowly, two or three digits a second. "C'mon, c'mon," he mumbled. Two cars roared down the street, blaring music.

Jim looked up from the pump as he heard voices. Three young men in matching black hoodies were cursing and talking in snarls as they approached the store. One of them cast a look in his direction. Jim quickly looked away and back at the pump. He was close to a half gallon. Two gallons should be just enough to get him home.

· · ·

The bells clanged loudly as the door to the store was thrown open. Malik looked over his shoulder again. His eyes widened slightly as he recognized the young men. It was Mike, Cam, and Tyrell from the local gang. He spun his back toward them and ducked his head.

Cam and Tyrell made their way in his direction. Mike remained up near the door, sorting through some candies.

"Good evening," Habib said. He continued to shelve the oil.

· · ·

Jim eyed the numbers on the gas pump. He tapped his foot and glanced back at the store. Through the big plate window hc could see the kids in hoodies spreading throughout the store. He frowned. One of the young men had just pocketed something off the shelf.

Just then, Jim's phone rang. He pulled it out of his coat. It was Mary Beth. He placed the phone back in his pocket. She'd have to wait until he was out of the cold and out of the neighborhood. She'd call back in a minute.

■　■　■

Mary Beth pulled the phone away from her ear. The call had gone straight to Jim's voicemail. She placed her finger over the redial button but then set the phone on the table with a sigh.

"He should be on the road by now," she said, shaking her head. She looked nervously back at her phone for a moment before walking briskly over to the refrigerator to get a bottle of water.

"Don't worry, Mary Beth," she whispered to herself. "He'll be fine—just give it a few more minutes . . ."

She took a quick swig from her bottle and stared back at the phone.

■　■　■

Malik breathed slowly. He could feel perspiration forming under his stocking cap. He needed them to leave. Tyrell rounded the aisle and stopped for a moment. Malik turned his head slightly and pretended to be looking at some energy drinks.

Habib rose slowly to his feet to keep an eye on his customers. Mike shuffled off around the corner. Tyrell stared hard at Malik and narrowed his eyes. "Yo, Cam," he said in a gravelly voice. "Who we got here?"

Cam squinted behind his glasses and shrugged.

Tyrell swatted his shoulder with the back of his hand. "I think that's Malik."

"Aye, is that you Malik?" Tyrell blurted out.

Malik kept his back turned to them. His heart and mind were racing. If he turned around, there would be no going back. He shot a glance to his left. Mike was between him and the exit. The milk in his hand felt like a gallon of lead. Habib, three aisles away, scratched the top of his head.

"You hear me talkin' to you?" Tyrell growled.

Malik reluctantly turned around to face his fear. As he did so, Tyrell flashed a menacing smile. Cam took another step forward.

"See?" Tyrell said as he slapped Cam's shoulder again. "I *told* you it was that clown, Malik. What'cha doin' in here, lil' punk?"

Malik swallowed and tried to gather his courage. "Grabbin' groceries for dinner."

"Yo, Mike," Tyrell hollered across the store. "Come here, dawg."

Mike rounded the corner with both of his hands jammed in his pockets. Malik was cornered.

Tyrell continued. "This is the dude I was tellin' you about who got a jump on Alonzo last week."

"That so?" Mike said.

"Aye!" Habib barked from across the store. "You guys need to chill out in here."

"Shut up, Osama!" Cam hollered. "This don't concern you."

The three teens closed in tightly around Malik. For a moment he entertained grabbing his gun, but he didn't like the odds. Running was the only option.

"Jumpin' one of our boys is like a death sentence, son," Mike said behind clenched teeth.

"I didn't jump your boy," Malik said as matter-of-factly as he could. "I got him off one of my boys. There's a difference."

Mike sneered and took another step forward. "You jumped one of our boys," he growled. "We ain't gonna let that pass."

Malik had to make his move soon. Another step and any one of them could put their hands on him. Fortunately, Habib made his move first. "That's it!" he said as he stormed back toward the cash register. "I'm calling the police."

"Will you get Mr. Taliban to shut up, please?" Mike growled at Tyrell.

Tyrell yanked open a refrigerator door and grabbed a bottle of beer before racing toward the cash register.

■ ■ ■

Jim glanced at the pump. Just a few more seconds. He looked back into the convenience store. The store manager was walking with swift and agitated steps toward the front of the store. He snatched the phone from the wall. One of the young men was right behind him.

■　■　■

Malik glanced desperately over at Habib. The store owner was dialing 911 with sharp jabs on his phone. In his haste, he hadn't latched the door to the bulletproof cashier box. Malik wanted to shout to warn his friend, but fear lodged his voice in his throat.

"Yes . . . hello . . . police . . ." Habib said. "Yes . . . I need for you—"

Tyrell dashed the bottle violently across the back of Habib's head. The old man collapsed to his knees. His phone fell to the ground with a crash. He released a moan as his trembling fingers reached for the blood streaming from his skull. Tyrell raised his hand and backhanded him, and Habib fell behind the counter. Malik grimaced at the dull thuds as the young man kicked him.

Mike and Cam were temporarily distracted by Tyrell. Malik lifted his gallon above his head and hurled it to the floor. It ruptured, providing the moment of shock that he needed. As Cam and Mike flinched from the explosion of icy milk, Malik darted past them and rounded the corner of the aisle. Tyrell made a desperate grab through the register door, but Malik was already past him.

Malik raced hard toward the doors and burst through them. He turned to his left and to his right. Mike and his

boys were shouting and cursing behind him. Outrunning
them was not an option. Then he saw the black Lexus.
A wide-eyed white man was ducking into the driver
seat. Malik bolted toward the car and reached for the
passenger door.

. . .

Jim fumbled for the door lock, but it was too late. Malik
had jumped inside. The two men looked at each other. Then
Jim's mouth widened: Malik's gun was in his hand. Malik
didn't remember pulling the gun out of his waistband, but
now it was pointed straight at Jim.

"C'mon, man!" Malik yelled as he half-ducked under
the dash. He held his gun near Jim's stomach. "Get us
outta here!"

Jim looked at the gun and then back out of the window.
Tyrell and Cam were standing just outside the store with
eyes full of fire. Sharp darts of breath shot from their
nostrils. Mike shoved them both aside and raced toward
the car.

"He's gonna kill us, man!" Malik pleaded with wide eyes.
"Let's go! Let's go!"

Jim was speechless. He fumbled wildly for his keys in
his coat pocket. Malik depressed the door lock just a second
before Mike snatched the handle. Mike angrily punched his
hand up against the window with a great thud.

Jim turned his key in the ignition and threw the car
into drive. Mike lurched backward as Jim accelerated

hard to his left, tires squealing, and merged back onto the main road.

■ ■ ■

Malik was crouched on the floorboard, his elbows on the seat. Beads of perspiration formed on his face. He was breathing heavily, and the gun was shaking in his trembling hand. Jim looked down at him.

"Where are we going?" Jim shouted. "What do I do? Please don't shoot me!"

Malik said nothing for a moment as he tried to get his bearings. "Just drive," he finally blurted. "Drive us far from here, man."

Jim continued down the main street toward the interstate. His whole body felt limp and numb; his foot on the pedal and his hands on the wheel scarcely gave him any sensations at all. He kept sucking in his lips and tightening his jaw. After a few blocks of silence, he decided to speak again.

"East or west?" he asked in a whisper.

"Huh?" Malik asked with a start.

"The interstate—do you want to go east or west?" Jim didn't know why he was asking these questions. He wanted to give Malik the keys and run away, but the neighborhood scared him. For some strange reason, being inside the car felt safer than anywhere else at the moment.

East would send them back to the suburbs, closer to Jim's home. West would take them out of the city.

"West," Malik mumbled. "Take us west."

■ ■ ■

As they pulled onto the interstate, Jim cast a glance into the rearview mirror. Home was getting farther away. He looked at the dash. The fuel indicator was one notch above "E." They wouldn't get more than fifty or sixty miles out of town before they had to fill up again. This fact filled him with a mixture of elation and horror.

Malik slowly raised himself up from crouching on the floorboard and sat down in the seat. He felt a drowning sense of hopelessness crashing down on him. He rubbed his hand up and down his face and sighed a great sigh.

Suddenly, the sense of panic reasserted itself. "Hey man! You want to go faster, dude?"

Jim was going ten miles under the speed limit. Cars were passing them with a whoosh. He applied his foot to the pedal, the car roared into action, and very shortly the city was just a yellowish glimmer on the skyline behind them. Nothing but vacant asphalt and distant taillights lay before them.

Malik leaned forward and clicked on the radio. He fumbled through a few stations hoping to hear some sort of update on what had just happened. He finally settled on a news station, but the commentator didn't say anything about the gas station—only a weather warning, the potential of freezing temperatures and possibly ice. His mind continued to race as his heart thumped wildly in his chest. He could imagine Mike, Cam, and Tyrell seething on some distant corner and plotting what they'd do to him when they found him. He could picture the police talking to eyewitnesses who were fingering him for mugging Habib. As they passed various cars and trucks on the road, he wondered if the other drivers knew who he was. Angst and fear consumed him.

Suddenly he slammed his fist against the dash and cursed. "This ain't right!" he blurted out. "I didn't do nothin'." He twisted violently in his seat, looking out every window. There were headlights in the distance behind them, two eighteen-wheelers not more than fifty yards ahead. Malik raised his gun just slightly in Jim's direction.

"Slow down a bit," he said. "Let these trucks get a ways ahead of us."

Malik's words were direct but wavering, with an underlying insecurity. He had no clue what he was doing.

"Look," Jim said cautiously, shooting a glance at Malik out of the corner of his eye. "You can just drop me off at the next exit and have the car." Now that Edgewood and gangbangers in hoodies were behind him, Jim was anxious to get out of this situation. He wondered if any witnesses back at the gas station would identify his car and somehow link him to the crime. He wanted to clear things up quickly. Getting away from Malik and his gun would be the first step toward making that happen.

Jim cleared his throat in an attempt to resurrect his offer, but Malik remained quiet. With white knuckles Jim gripped the steering wheel. The clock on the dash said 6:27. He grimaced. He should be pulling into his garage right now.

Instead he was plunging further into the dark night down some desolate stretch of highway.

Just then, Jim's cell phone rang. The noise itself startled both men like an explosion. Malik raised his gun from his lap.

"Who . . . who is that?" Malik asked aggressively.

"It's probably my wife," Jim replied. "I was supposed to be home, like, ten minutes ago. She's wondering where I am."

Malik hesitated for a moment. The phone continued to ring in Jim's coat pocket. His eyes narrowed.

"Just let it go," Malik offered.

"She'll keep calling," Jim said with a nervous chuckle. "She's like that."

The ringing stopped, and the car was filled with silence. But then, only ten seconds later, the ringing resumed.

"I told you," Jim mumbled. "She won't give up till I answer. She's a persistent woman."

"Fine!" Malik barked. "You answer it, but tell her you're broke down. Then you tell her about the tow truck that's on its way. Then you tell her about how hard it is to hear her and that you'll call her back when you know somethin'."

"I can't lie to my wife."

"Man, bump lying, dude!" Malik growled as he gripped his gun. "You'll do what I say. I ain't gettin' arrested or shot for a bunch of nonsense—you got me?"

Jim nodded. He reached slowly into his coat pocket and pulled out his phone. He glanced at Malik's desperate eyes and the gun in his hand before answering the call. "Uh, hi honey." His voice cracked slightly.

Malik leaned his ear close to Jim's face, struggling to hear the conversation. Jim grimaced and spoke with as much confidence as he could muster. "Yeah . . . I had some car troubles. I broke down about ten minutes after dropping those groceries off . . . I'm waiting for the wrecker now . . ."

Jim stopped talking as his wife shouted her dismay. He glanced at Malik with a look of embarrassment.

"Yes . . . yes, honey, I'm out of the neighborhood . . . I'm safe now . . . No! Listen to me, your dad doesn't need to come get me. I'll call you when I know something."

"Tell her you can't hear her anymore," Malik hissed as he leaned forward. "You'll call her later, remember?"

"Baby, I can't hear you anymore. It's breaking up awful. I'll call you in an hour or two. I love you. I gotta go," Jim said through a clenched jaw. With a great effort he pulled the phone from his face and clicked it off.

"Here. Gimme that," Malik said as he yanked it from Jim's grasp. Without hesitation he rolled down the window and hurled the phone down against the asphalt. Jim watched in dismay as the phone disintegrated into bouncing bits in the rearview mirror.

Malik's phone chirped. He carefully slid it out of his pocket and took a look. It was a text from Brenden. *Tell me u ain't caught up in that mess @ the gas station. Some folks r puttin ur name out there.*

Malik felt sick. He slowly pulled his hat off his head and dragged his hand across his forehead. His grandmother's ten-dollar bill fell to the floorboard between his feet. He looked out the window. Dense woods lurked in the distance. The sky was speckled with stars. The moon hung like a bright white dish. For a moment he thought about his grandmother and the Thanksgiving dinner she'd be preparing in the next couple of days. His chin dropped on his chest. The gun in his lap felt like a boulder. He stared hard at the floor.

"We gotta get off this road," he said with resignation. "Take the next exit and get us somewhere else."

"I don't understand," Jim replied. "What's the plan? I already told you, just drop me off somewhere and take the car."

Malik cast his eyes on Jim. They were resolute. "I ain't got no plan," Malik said. "Just do what I said and get us off this road. Now!"

Jim's head was spinning. Why wouldn't this kid just let him go? What was he thinking?

A road sign in the distance indicated that county highway 57 was two miles ahead. "Take 57," Malik said, pointing at the sign. "That'll work."

7

THE COLD

7:15 p.m., Monday before Thanksgiving

THE COUNTRY ROAD WAS DARK AND OMINOUS. Aside from a full moon that played peek-a-boo behind wispy gray clouds and a towering wall of pine trees, the high beams from the Lexus were the only lights in the night. The asphalt glistened in front of them like an ebony carpet speckled with jewels. Thin drops of sleet peppered the front windshield.

Jim grimaced, gripping the steering wheel. He glanced at the dash. It was 7:15 and twenty-six degrees outside. He knew his wife had kept calling, even though he had told her not to. It was only a matter of time before she would start to panic, if she hadn't already. But what could she do? How could she—or anyone, for that matter—find him? His stomach churned.

He stole a glance at the kid in his passenger seat and at

the gun resting in his lap. *Is this thug going to kill me out here?* He didn't seem like a killer, but Jim couldn't be certain. And anyway, even if the kid let him go now, how would he survive in this freezing wilderness? All he had was a fleece and no phone. Death was possible both inside and outside his vehicle, and he was powerless to change the outcome in either scenario.

Malik sat in the passenger seat, angry. He felt like a puppy fleeing from a wolf, only to find a tiger hindering his escape. Where could he go? What could he do? He had only driven a car a few times when his Uncle Keith was trying to help him get his permit a couple of years ago. He wouldn't feel comfortable driving this car on a night like this. He couldn't let this man go, even though he had offered Malik the car. And he couldn't just let the man drop him off. He had no good options.

The road took a sharp turn ahead. Jim decelerated and kept both hands on the wheel as he prepared to navigate the curve, but the back tires hissed and fishtailed slightly on the slick blacktop. Malik grabbed the door handle and cursed under his breath.

"That's ice, kid," Jim blurted out. As the road straightened, the car righted itself. "It's not safe on this road. It's freezing outside, and this sleet is going to continue to stick and ice over. We need to stop somewhere before we end up in a ditch!"

Malik knew the man was right—the road was becoming more dangerous by the minute. He also knew that the 9mm in his lap meant that he was in charge, and as precarious as the road was becoming, driving still felt right. Moving felt right. The idea of stopping anywhere frightened him more than anything.

"Just keep going for a while," Malik muttered.

Jim shot a look of disbelief at his captor. He let out a sigh and kept driving.

After five minutes of silence the low-fuel light came on again. Jim's stomach sank. "Do you see that?" he asked as he jabbed his finger at the dash. "That light right there means we need to stop somewhere soon, or this car is going to stop for us."

"Man, you think I don't know what that light means?" Malik blurted. "So where do you want to stop, huh? You got some place in mind? Ain't nothing out here but trees and darkness."

Jim was driving under twenty miles per hour, doing his best to stay on the slick road. The sleet was falling in thick sheets now, freezing to the windshield. He adjusted the heat and threw on his wipers. They crossed a short bridge, and the car fishtailed again. An old wooden sign along the side of the road referenced a hunting camp three miles up the road.

Both men noticed the sign at the same time. They made eye contact for a moment.

"I think we found ourselves a place to stop," Jim said hopefully. "A couple nights before Thanksgiving, I doubt anyone will be there. I bet we can find a cabin to hole up in for the night."

Malik hated every bit of this idea, but the icy roads and the yellow dash light gave them no options. One bad patch of ice would send them off the road and into even greater danger. They hadn't passed another vehicle in over thirty minutes. Help wouldn't be coming.

"Fine. Whatever," Malik said resignedly. He shook his head.

"There's probably some firewood . . . maybe some food," Jim said wishfully.

"Bet you there's some rednecks with dogs and guns too," Malik mumbled.

"Hey," Jim replied, "I'll take rednecks and dogs over dying of hypothermia in a ditch any day."

"Not me," Malik said tersely. "Just let me freeze."

Suddenly, a sharp wind rushed across the road and barreled violently into the car, like an invisible monster. Jim tried to steady the wheel as the vehicle slid slowly like a puck on the ice.

"Dang!" Malik braced one hand on the dash.

Ahead was another sharp curve. Flecks of ice and snow twisted across the road like snakes. Jim took his foot off the gas to navigate the turn, but a large dip in the road sent the car into a free skid toward the road's edge. The vehicle lights revealed a precarious rocky slope just six feet beyond the road.

"Hold on!" Jim shouted, more to himself than anyone else. The car skidded past the edge of the road and toward the ledge until the thick dead grass snagged and stopped them.

The two men paused for a minute to catch their breath. Malik slowly looked out of the passenger window and eyed the jagged slope, just two feet outside of his car door.

"I guess a hunting cabin may be the safer option," he said faintly.

Jim peeled his hands from the steering wheel and ran them through his hair. He looked at the young man beside him and nodded before slowly hitting the gas pedal and steering them over the grassy patch and back onto the road.

■ ■ ■

From that moment on, the two drove in silence. Occasionally they both shot glances at the gas light. Soon, though, they saw the sign for Morgan's Hunting Cabins and an arrow pointing to the left. Jim took the turn. The sound of gravel under his tires reassured him, and he relaxed his grip on the steering wheel.

Malik had never been this far from the city in his life. The pop of the gravel under the car was unnerving, a sound he had never heard before. The road was narrow, and the trees leered over the vehicle, their leafless branches reaching out like menacing arms.

To their right, nestled back in the trees, was a small cabin. An old pickup truck was parked beside it. Malik squinted into the darkness. He thought he spotted a faint light in one of the windows, but he couldn't be sure. They continued on and passed more cabins. Dark and vacant, they sat back among the trees. Jim was about to offer a suggestion that they pick a place when suddenly Malik chimed in. "That's the one! Park the car in the back."

Jim was surprised by the young man's enthusiasm, but he followed his lead. The drive leading toward this cabin was wide, and the cabin itself wasn't shrouded by as many trees the way the other ones were. Jim didn't understand the excitement, but he was ready to get out of the car.

"Turn here and then back it in behind the house," Malik said.

Jim did as he was told. Behind the cabin was a rear entrance and, to Jim's elation, a small stack of firewood underneath a tattered tarp. For the first time he felt that he might survive the night after all.

8

THE INVESTIGATION

8:45 p.m., Monday before Thanksgiving

MARQUAN LOOKED AGAIN AT THE ADDRESS ON HIS NOTEPAD: 1017 Spencer Road. The light turned green, and he took a left up the hill into Stone Brook. The roads were almost completely empty. The cold and the threat of ice had people behind doors. He took a sip of his coffee and meandered slowly up the hill. He eyed the gated mansions and their long, bricked driveways.

"Some big houses for some big-time people," he said with a half-smile.

He threw on his blinker and turned onto Spencer Road. Driving slowly with his head cocked sideways, he tried to find the street numbers along the gates and walls surrounding the houses he passed.

"1013 . . . 1015 . . . 1017—there you are," he mumbled.

"Ah, and the gate is open too. Why, thank you very much."
He cruised slowly up the driveway and parked next to a
black Mercedes SUV. The front door to the house opened,
casting light out into the spacious front yard. Detective Cole
took a final sip of his coffee as a silver-haired man in a dark
blue sweater and khakis stared at him from the entrance.
MarQuan opened the door and stepped out into the night.

"Evening, Congressman Lawrey," the detective said,
waving his hand in the air. "I'm Detective MarQuan Cole—"

The older man frowned. "Where's Detective Podolski?
I called for him."

MarQuan shook his head and smiled. "He's gone for the
holiday, sir. Is your daughter home? And if so, may I come in?"

Just then Mary Beth appeared in the door. Her father
slung his arm around her and pulled her close. Her eyes were
red, and she held a wad of tissues in her fist.

"Yes . . . yes, of course. Come in, Detective." The congressman beckoned MarQuan in with some terse waves of his hand.

"Thank you, sir," MarQuan said as he walked up the stone
steps. He squinted slightly in the bright lights of the living
room. He took a few moments to wipe his feet on the mat at
the door. "You have a nice place, ma'am," he said cheerfully.

"Come in, Detective," the congressman said without
smiling. "This is my daughter, Mary Beth. Over there is my
wife, Susan."

MarQuan stepped inside. Susan was seated in a small
chair at the back of the room, frowning and gazing absently
at the flames crackling away in the fireplace. He took one

more minute to survey the house from where he stood, admiring the high ceilings and the large painting of a flowery field just above the hearth. He nodded slightly and then turned his attention to Mary Beth.

"Do you mind if I have a seat?" MarQuan asked, sitting down in a cozy leather recliner. He removed his notepad from his coat pocket and plucked a pen from behind his ear. "So, since your phone call came in, Congressman, we've done a little bit of homework at the precinct." He crossed his legs.

Mary Beth and her father sat down on a couch opposite from the detective. Susan shifted her head slightly to hear better, even though she continued to stare into the fire.

"You said your husband called two hours ago and said he was broke down somewhere en route to coming home?" MarQuan read the details from his notes. "And now his calls go straight to voice mail?"

Mary Beth nodded.

"There have been a handful of accidents and cars broken down along the interstate tonight," MarQuan said matter-of-factly, "but no black Lexus. The roads, as you know, are getting bad, but the weather is a lot worse northwest of us." He cleared his throat. "Where was your husband? Was he coming home from work?"

Mary Beth shook her head. "He was in Edgewood."

The detective's eyes widened. "Edgewood! What was he doing over there?"

"Trying to be a Good Samaritan," the congressman said with a slight growl.

"I don't understand."

Mary Beth sighed. "Our Sunday school class has this little ministry for some struggling family over there . . . I don't know . . . We drop off groceries once a week for an old lady and her grandkids or something like that. Jim and I don't go. We just give food or whatever. But this time Jim had to go because no one else would."

"I see." MarQuan nodded.

"I told him not to go," Mary Beth continued. "It's Thanksgiving week, my parents were coming in, and besides, that neighborhood is . . ." Mary Beth looked at Detective Cole for a moment, trying to choose her words carefully.

"It's full of thugs, drugs, guns, and robbers!" Mary Beth's mother spun away from the fire. "It's enough that we have ISIS and Al Qaeda in the world, but now we've got our own little Baghdad just twenty minutes down the road! What was he thinking, Mary Beth?"

MarQuan looked over at Mary Beth. She was blotting her eyes with her tissue. "I don't know, Mama," she whispered softly.

"Doesn't he watch the news?" her mother continued as her hands trembled in her lap. "Every night there's another shooting, another kid getting killed, some crack house burning down. That's no place for a man like Jim!"

"Jim's a smart man," the congressman muttered. "He knows better. Decent folks don't go to Edgewood— particularly at night. My job used to take me down there years ago, back when I worked for the power company. I used to keep a gun in my glove box just in case."

MarQuan smiled slightly. "My grandmother still lives in Edgewood. I grew up near there. It's a pretty tough neighborhood, for sure." Mary Beth and her parents looked uncomfortably at him for a moment but said nothing.

MarQuan flipped a page on his notepad and continued. "The only leaf that we've turned over was an incident at a convenience store down there, about three hours ago. Video footage shows some teenagers arguing about something in the store, and then one of them assaulted the cashier when he tried to call the police. He's in critical condition. There are no cameras outside, but a witness in the parking lot says she saw one of the teenagers pull a gun and flee in a black Lexus sedan."

Congressman Lawrey looked aghast. "You don't think that was Jim? You think a successful attorney like him is going to start knocking over gas stations like some sort of street thug? He's a good man with a good life, detective. I hope that you have more to go on than that!"

MarQuan shrugged. "I've seen stranger things, sir. Anyway, I'm not saying that your son-in-law was involved in the incident. The footage never puts him in the store. Maybe it was a carjacking, or maybe it was someone else altogether."

"Carjacking?" Mary Beth said with a slight gasp.

"We need to entertain every possibility, ma'am. At this point it's all that we really have to go on." MarQuan took a few sharp jabs at his notepad with his pen. "I have to ask," he said reluctantly. "Were you and Jim having any marital trouble—or was he having any other kind of trouble?"

Mary Beth's father cleared his throat obnoxiously as his daughter answered. "No. Why?"

"I had to ask. You'll have to excuse me, but a man from this neighborhood bringing groceries to Edgewood sounds a bit unlikely. Is there anyone in Edgewood that could verify he was there?"

Mary Beth glowered. "We don't know anyone in Edgewood." She nodded toward an adjacent room. "There's a sheet of paper that had the old lady's name and address on it. Our Sunday school leader gave it to Jim yesterday when he found out Jim was the one going down there. I think it's on Jim's desk."

"I'll get it, honey," her father said. He hurried off toward his son-in-law's office.

"So," MarQuan continued. "How did you and your husband get to know this . . . old lady?" He shifted his weight in the chair.

Mary Beth pursed her lips and shook her head. "We don't know her—she works at our church. One of the cleaning ladies, I think."

"Why do you bring her food?"

Mary Beth sighed. "I guess our Sunday school class has been bringing stuff down there for a couple months now."

"But you don't know her?"

"Her name is Wilma Thompson," Congressman Lawrey said as he stormed back into the room. He was reading off a piece of paper in his hand. "She lives at 917 42nd Street. Eastbrook Apartments . . . Apartment 3G." He handed the paper to Detective Cole and sat back down by his daughter.

"Wilma Thompson, you say?" MarQuan knew that name.

The congressman pointed at the paper. "That's what it says."

MarQuan looked over the paper. "Westside Hope, huh?" He looked up at Mary Beth. "Is that what you call your church's food dropoffs? Interesting. Do you mind if I keep this?"

Mary Beth shook her head, and MarQuan stood to his feet. "Well, this is helpful. We'll get over to talk with Ms. Thompson. Do you happen to have a picture of Jim that I could take with me?"

"Sure," Mary Beth said. She got up and walked over to an oak cabinet by the front door. She rummaged through it for a minute until she found a stack of pictures. She selected one and handed it to MarQuan.

"Thank you," he said. He gave the picture a quick glance and then tucked it in his jacket pocket. "I really should be going. We'll find Jim, ma'am. Don't you worry." He left his card on the end table. "Call me if you need anything else."

The congressman rose off the couch and opened the door for him. "Good night, detective."

Detective Cole stepped outside and shuddered as the cold breeze lashed against his skin. "Y'all stay warm and safe tonight." The door shut behind him.

9

THE CABIN

9:37 p.m., Monday before Thanksgiving

JIM LOOKED AT THE DASH. It was 9:37 and nineteen degrees outside. He turned off the engine and put the key in a console on his dash. Malik looked out of the window and frowned. "Man, this looks like the home of a serial killer for real!" He pulled his stocking cap back on his head.

Jim looked over at his teenaged captor. This change in plans had suddenly swung the night in his favor. He looked down at the gun that Malik held in his lap and decided to open the car door.

"Come on!" Jim said. The frigid air invaded the inside of the car in a matter of seconds. "You'll freeze out here in no time."

Malik inhaled a deep breath, summoning his courage, and opened the passenger door. Jim was already at the back of the cabin. He opened the rickety-screened door, raised his hands, and gave the back door a quick but loud knock.

"Yo, what're you doing, man?" Malik said. He raised his gun, which was shaking in his cold, nervous hands.

"Look," Jim said plainly. "The quickest way for us both to get killed tonight is to barge into the middle of a hunting cabin uninvited. Put your gun down—I'm just seeing if anybody is home."

Malik lowered his weapon slightly, but he remained tense as Jim gave the door one more knock. They waited quietly for a moment.

"I don't think anyone's here," Jim said. "Let's get inside." He tried the main door, and to their surprise it was unlocked.

Jim stepped inside first. It smelled like cigarette smoke and dust. "You got a light on that phone of yours?" Jim asked hopefully.

Malik pulled his cell phone out of his pocket and glanced at it with a frown. "I got a light but no signal out here." He turned his phone on and held it high. The screen provided a faint light. They could make out an old table with three chairs in the middle of the room. Up against the far wall were two bunk beds with a window between them.

Jim suddenly disappeared into the darkness. "Man, hold up," Malik said loudly. "Where you goin'?"

"Bring that light over here," Jim said from somewhere to Malik's right. Malik followed Jim's voice slowly until he saw him standing next to a fireplace.

"This right here is the key to survival," Jim said.

"Cool. But how are you going to light a fire?"

"I think I have some matches in the car."

The air inside the cabin wasn't much warmer than outside. Jim and Malik could both feel their fingers growing numb. Jim raised his hands to his mouth and fired a few puffs of hot breath into them before rubbing them together. "All right, let's see here." He turned slowly. On one of the mattresses was an old newspaper. "Shine that light in the fireplace," he told Malik as he grabbed the newspaper.

Malik met him in front of the fireplace and stuck his phone out to fill it with light. "Nothing but ashes and some ol' beer cans," he said ruefully. Jim started wadding up sheets of the newspaper. "Man," Malik scoffed, "how long you think that little newspaper is gonna keep us warm? Like maybe one minute . . ."

"This little newspaper is a godsend," Jim said. He got down on his knees and started arranging the wads of paper in the base of the fireplace.

"How so?" Malik asked.

Jim looked up at Malik. "Didn't you see the stack of firewood outside? I'll hopefully have a good fire going here in just a minute. Tell you what, why don't you get out there and grab some of the smallest logs you can find and bring them back in here?"

"You crazy?" Malik replied. "I ain't going out there in the dark by myself. It's cold and scary out there."

Jim sighed. "Fine. I'll go get the logs. You keep wadding up newspaper and placing it in there the way I've got it."

Malik mumbled something under his breath, got down on his knees, and grabbed a sheet of newspaper. Jim stood there awkwardly for almost fifteen seconds before he cleared his throat. "You mind if I have the light?" he asked tersely.

"How am I supposed to do what I'm doin' if you got my light?" Malik retorted over his shoulder.

Jim was getting angry. "I need to see what types of logs to grab so that I can start a fire and stay alive! Now give me the light or let's go do it together. Either way, I need to see what I'm doing."

Malik paused for a minute and then jumped to his feet. "Whatever, man. Let's just go do this together then. I ain't stayin' here in the dark. You'll probably jump in your ride and leave my behind here to freeze."

Jim said nothing. He turned and started walking back toward the door.

Malik shook his head and followed. He carefully placed his gun back in the waistband of his pants.

Once they were outside Jim pulled back the tarp. "Shine the light right here."

Malik walked up next to him and placed his phone in front of the log heap. Jim studied the pile for a moment and then snatched some twigs, branches, and a few small pieces of kindling wood. "This will do to get us started." He turned back to the cabin, with Malik at his heels.

The two of them crouched down at the fireplace. Under the dim light of the cell phone, Jim cracked some of the twigs and arranged them like a teepee around the packed wad of newspapers. He set some of the smaller pieces of wood off to the side. Malik watched curiously. He had never seen anyone build a fire before.

Jim clapped his hands and stood to his feet. "And now for the moment of truth. Time to get those matches." He looked at Malik for a few moments with an annoyed smile. "I guess we'll go get that together too, huh?"

■ ■ ■

Jim struck a match and cupped it in his hands like a precious jewel. The flame flickered precariously as he stretched his arms toward the fireplace. He was able to light a few edges of the crumpled wads of paper. He leaned forward and blew softly. The paper brightened, and suddenly a substantial flame emerged. Some of the twigs started to pop and crackle. Malik let out a quiet whistle.

"Almost in business now," Jim said. Slowly and carefully he placed some of the smaller pieces of kindling onto the teepee of twigs. The heat from the slight fire rushed against them, and they immediately placed their numbed and desperate fingers just inches from the undulating flames. They crouched there like this until they could feel their hands again.

"Thank God!" Jim said loudly as he got back to his feet. "Now it's time to get some real logs. I'm going to need that light."

Malik looked longingly at the fire and then at his phone for a moment. After a pause he sighed and stood up also. "Let's go." He led the way this time.

It wasn't long until they had transitioned all of the logs inside and had a robust fire roaring away. Jim grabbed them each a chair from the table, and they sat there huddled around the flames. The heat cascaded over them with warmth and life. Jim looked Malik over for a moment. It was the first occasion he had really taken a look at his unusual company. Malik was just a kid.

■ ■ ■

As Malik stared into the flames, he realized that this was the first time in hours that he felt remotely safe. The cold outside could kill him, but it was also a barrier between him and everything else that frightened him. Mike and his gang. The police. The cold was a monster on a bridge: It wouldn't let him leave, but neither would it allow anything else across to harm him. And for the time being, that gave him peace.

10

THE VISIT

9:55 p.m., Monday before Thanksgiving

MARQUAN PULLED OFF THE INTERSTATE into Edgewood. It was almost 10:00 p.m. The parking lots at the convenience stores were almost all vacant. The storm had pushed west of the city, but it was still below freezing outside. Soft blues music played on his radio as he nursed another cup of coffee and rolled slowly through the neighborhood. He looked at the dilapidated houses along the edge of the street. The bright flashes of televisions danced behind the drawn curtains.

"Nothing like the cold and snow to keep the bad guys indoors," he mumbled to himself with a slight grin. "Old Edgewood is a ghost town tonight."

He turned onto 42nd Street and made his way toward the Eastbrook apartment complex. An Edgewood police car was parked out front. He parked his car on the opposite curb. *I hope Ms. Thompson is still awake*, he thought. He slammed his car door shut and shrugged his way through the cold to apartment 3G.

MarQuan could hear a muffled conversation taking place inside. As he knocked, the voices stopped. Slow, small footsteps approached the door. Someone inside fumbled with the handle. The door opened slightly, and a little boy peered at him through the crack.

"Good evening, son. Is Ms. Thompson here? My name is Detective Cole." He offered a reassuring smile.

The boy stared at him for a moment and then hollered over his shoulder, "Grandma! There's a detective man here to see you."

"Can you let him in, baby?" a woman replied from the back of the apartment.

Detective Cole smiled as the boy opened the door for him to enter. He walked slowly down the short hallway and smiled again when he spotted the picture of a man in military fatigues. As he rounded the corner, he saw an elderly woman seated in the corner of her couch. Two large white policemen towered over her.

"Ms. Thompson?" he said with a slight wave. The woman nodded. The two officers took a step backward and stared at him as he entered the room.

"Good evening, ma'am," he said. He nodded at the officers and flashed his badge. "I'm Detective MarQuan Cole from the Stone Brook precinct. You probably don't remember me, but I was friends with your son Keith back in the day."

Ms. Thompson looked at him for a moment and studied his face, but then she shook her head.

"I'm sorry, hon, I don't remember you," she said regretfully.

"He and I served in Iraq—did two tours together. He was a good soldier and a great man." Detective Cole's voice trailed off slightly as he looked at Ms. Thompson. "I heard about his accident a couple of years ago . . . I'm very sorry. How is he?"

She grimaced. "Keith is making it one day at a time, I suppose."

"I'm Officer Briggs," one of the policemen interrupted. "This is my partner, Officer Jenkins."

Detective Cole cleared his throat. "It looks like you're already having a busy night. I was wondering if I could ask you a couple of questions."

Ms. Thompson's face furled into some wrinkles, and she shook her head slightly. "I suppose you're here about Malik also."

Detective Cole frowned, a look of confusion on his face. "Malik? No ma'am, I'm here about—"

"We're here about the incident that took place over at the gas station down the road," Officer Briggs interrupted again. MarQuan's eyes widened.

"Did I hear you say to Ms. Thompson that you're from Stone Brook?" Officer Jenkins scratched his nose as he spoke. "This seems a little outside of your stomping grounds, doesn't it?"

Detective Cole smiled and pulled the picture that Mary Beth had given him out of his pocket. "Ms. Thompson, have you seen this man before?" He handed it to her.

Ms. Thompson put on her glasses and studied the picture. Her face brightened. "Why yes. That's Jim Dawkins. He brought us some groceries for Thanksgiving tonight. Why?"

MarQuan noticed the three children huddled together on the floor under a blanket, watching cartoons in the corner of the room. "Do you think they could go in another room?" he asked softly. "It would be good for us to talk."

"Monique, baby, it's time for bed," Ms. Thompson called out. "Please help your brother and sister brush their teeth and then go lie down in my room, okay, honey?"

The older girl nodded and clicked off the television. "Come on, y'all." They exited the room, and MarQuan motioned for the elderly woman to sit down. He sat down beside her and turned his attention to the two policemen, standing awkwardly in the middle of the room. "So, what do you have, officers?" he asked.

Officer Briggs looked down at his notepad. "Ms. Thompson called the police about thirty or forty minutes ago, claiming that her grandson, Malik, was missing. We believe that it's possible he was involved in an assault that took place at the gas station earlier this evening. She indicated to us that she had sent him there for some groceries and that he never came home. A witness in the parking lot says that there were four people inside the store besides the owner. All four were wearing hoodies, so the witness couldn't identify anyone. Three fled on foot. One fled in a black Lexus sedan."

"Jim Dawkins drives a black Lexus sedan," MarQuan said.

Ms. Thompson shook her head. "My baby wouldn't hurt or rob nobody. He's not like that—"

"Of course he wouldn't," Officer Jenkins mumbled.

MarQuan pulled out his notepad. "Did Malik know Jim?"

"No. They've never met before. Jim arrived here a few minutes after Malik left to get me the milk and butter."

"How do you know Jim?"

"I just met him for the first time today," she replied. "People from his church—well, it's actually the church where I work—they've been bringing us groceries for the last month or two."

"So you and your grandson have no relationship whatsoever with Jim Dawkins?"

"No."

"The timeline puts Malik at the gas station at the time of the assault," Jenkins interjected, trying to change the subject.

Ms. Thompson balled up her tiny fists. "I'm tellin' you he wouldn't hurt nobody. Habib is a friend of his. He's known that man all his life."

"He's run before, Ms. Thompson," Briggs said. "This isn't his first time to do something stupid and run. You don't think it's suspicious that he was there when all of this happened, and now he's just vanished?"

Ms. Thompson looked up at the officer with a pained expression. MarQuan spoke up for her. "What are you suggesting?"

"He has two priors," Briggs said, looking at Ms. Thompson. "One for theft and one for possession. When he was caught stealing, he took off running and was apprehended a few blocks down the road."

"He was barely ten years old then," the woman said desperately. "He was a boy and he was scared. Some friends dared him to steal some candy bars, and when the police showed up he got scared and ran."

"And the marijuana?" Jenkins said. He rested his hands on his hips.

"Foolishness," she replied. "About four years ago he got mixed up with some boys that smoke. A lot of boys smoke that nasty stuff. But he doesn't do it anymore."

"It's in his nature," Briggs said. "He was involved in what happened tonight. He's 'missing' for a reason. We need to find him and ask him some questions."

"Where do you think he could be?" Jenkins asked.

Ms. Thompson dropped her head and shrugged. "I tried to call him for the last couple of hours but it just goes to his voice mail. I called his best friend, and he said he hasn't seen him tonight. I tried to call his mama's house too. I don't know where he is." A few tears emerged in her aged eyes. MarQuan wanted to place a hand on her shoulder but thought better of it.

"Covering for your grandson isn't going to help!" Briggs

was suddenly impatient. "Protecting him is only going to make all of this worse."

"Why do you think I'd call y'all if I was covering for him?" she replied. "Now what kinda sense does that make?"

"Ms. Thompson," MarQuan asked softly. "Where's Malik's mother?"

She sniffed, shook her head, and stared at the floor.

"His mama," Briggs said as he rolled his neck, "has a good rap sheet of her own. Two counts of possession, incident of public intoxication, and some other fun stuff. Like I said, it's in his nature—apples don't fall far from the tree."

MarQuan glared at the policeman and cleared his throat. "Sounds like you two almost have this whole thing figured out." He turned his attention back to the woman. "Ma'am, we need to find Malik. Jim Dawkins has gone missing as well. I spoke with his wife earlier this evening. She has no idea where he is. Do you have any idea at all where he might be?"

Ms. Thompson continued to stare at the floor and dab at her eyes and nose with a handkerchief.

"Detective," Jenkins asked cautiously, "are we dealing with more than the assault incident at the gas station?"

MarQuan sighed and stood to his feet. "I don't know." He took a look at his watch. "What I do know is that we're about nineteen hours away from having to fill out two missing-persons reports."

THE INTRODUCTIONS

10:15 p.m., Monday before Thanksgiving

MALIK HELD HIS HANDS OUT in front of the fire for a moment and let the heat warm his palms before he stuffed them back in his pockets. They had stacked all of the logs between their chairs. The flames cast shadows that danced eerily on the walls around them. Tiny snowflakes pelted the windows. He looked over at Jim, who was staring into the fireplace as if he were in a trance. The silence, like the darkness, was suffocating.

"So what do you do, man?" Malik asked.

Malik's voice entered into Jim's wandering mind and shook him like a man roused from a deep sleep. "Huh?" Jim replied. "What'd you say?"

"I mean, what do you do for a job? You must have a nice job driving a car like that."

"I'm a lawyer."

"Dope." Malik shrugged. "Let me guess—you live up in Meadow Glade?"

"No." Jim paused. "Stone Brook."

Malik whistled and shook his head. "Wow! A lawyer from Stone Brook. You ballin', ain't you, man?"

Jim felt disoriented by the conversation. He chose to poke the fire with a stick instead of responding. But Malik wasn't finished. "So why were you in Edgewood, man? You there for a taste or somethin'?"

"A taste?"

"Why were you in Edgewood?" Malik repeated. "There aren't too many dudes that look like you in my neighborhood for real—unless they're lookin' for some particular purchases."

Jim looked confused. "Particular purchases? What's that mean?"

"Come on, man!" Malik said with a smirk. "I ain't stupid. White dudes like you don't roll into Edgewood unless they're cops or they're lookin' for drugs or some sexual healing."

Jim frowned. "It's not like that. I was dropping off some groceries for an old lady and her grandkids."

Malik was silent for a moment, and then he burst out laughing. "Wait! What? Were you bringing groceries to Wilma Thompson?"

Jim nodded.

"Are you from Mars, man?"

"Yeah—I attend Mars Chapel. Why? How'd you know that?"

Malik shook his head in disbelief.

"What is it?" Jim asked again.

"Man . . ." Malik looked Jim in the eye. "Wilma Thompson is my grandmama."

Jim's face was shrouded with confusion.

"I'm Malik," he said softly. "I'm her grandson."

Jim remained silent for a moment. Then he cleared his throat. "I'm Jim—Jim Dawkins. I'd shake your hand, but you kidnapped me with a gun, broke my phone, got me lost in the middle of nowhere. So . . ."

Malik ignored him. "Did you deliver the groceries, or are they still in your trunk? I'm starving."

"No," Jim replied. "They're at your grandma's house. I brought y'all stuff for Thanksgiving dinner."

Malik pursed his lips and looked back out the window. "Well, man, this is messed up, isn't it?" He watched as a log popped a lone coal out onto the hearth. "I bet you wish now you had kept all that food and stayed home tonight, don't you? Now you're in the middle of nowhere, stuck with a kid with a gun, freezing your butt off. Bet you didn't see that one coming."

"My wife told me to stay home." Jim was getting more irritated by the minute. "I should've listened to her."

Malik flashed a wry grin. "She didn't want you in the dangerous neighborhood at night, did she? Too many thugs with guns? Usually you people do your food drop when it's light out. Then you shoot your selfies with the smiling and grateful black kids and roll home. Hopefully you at least got your picture with Jamal. He loves to smile. Did you get your pictures, man?"

Jim frowned. "It's not like that. I thought you liked the food. Someone said your grandma needed some help. We're just trying to help."

"Yeah?" Malik asked. "Who told you we needed help? Pam and Sammy?"

"Pat and Sally," Jim corrected him.

"Whatever," Malik replied. "Did they tell you that?"

Jim's lips tightened. "Yes they did."

"And where'd they get their info from?" A surprising burst of bold anger emerged as Malik spoke. "Let me ask you this—before today have you ever met my grandma?"

Jim shook his head.

"So how do you know that we need groceries, then?"

"Well—do you?" Jim fired back.

Malik shrugged. "Even if we did, have any of you people ever asked us *what* we want to eat? Let me tell you something, man. People in my neighborhood don't like hummus, dude. That stuff tastes like dirt. But I guess y'all think everybody likes it, because we get a tub of the nasty stuff every week."

Jim could feel his temper rising. "So, are you saying you guys don't want the food? Because I can talk to Pat and Sally and we can end that tomorrow."

"What I'm saying," Malik said, "is that I don't want to be your charity case. You ain't helping us for real. I mean, look at us right now, dude. We could freeze here in the next day or so if someone doesn't find us, right?"

Jim nodded.

Malik continued. "Well, what if someone drives by in a few hours in a big ol' truck and they see us. But instead of getting us out of here they just throw us a blanket, take a picture with us, and then drive off. How'd you feel?"

"I don't get it," Jim growled.

"Man, if the dude in the truck really cared, he'd get us up out of here. A blanket ain't gonna help us for real. Plus it's disrespectful for a dude to do that when he could do so much more."

"So, what are you saying?" Jim snapped. "Do you want us to bring food every day, except punt on the hummus?"

"I think you're missing the whole point, man. We don't need your charity. How about giving my grandma a job where she could actually take care of herself? How about treating her like she *is* somebody. We don't need your groceries. My grandma would like to buy her own groceries with her own money. You feel me?"

"What's that got to do with me?" Jim asked. "You want me to find her a job or something?"

"How long have you been at Mars, huh?"

"Since I was about five or six," Jim replied. "So for almost thirty years. Why?"

"Because," Malik said, "my grandma has been working there for thirty-six years. Do you know what she does there?"

Jim sighed loudly. "I don't know. I'm guessing she works in maintenance or something, right?"

"Yessir." Malik slapped his hands on his thighs. "You got

it! She's been scrubbing your toilets, vacuuming your carpets, and cleaning up your messes for longer than you've been alive. Man, there's been like five different pastors up there since she started working. But all that time she makes a sorry ten bucks an hour. Now y'all got a pastor up there who's barely thirty, and he's making more money in a year than my grandma can make in six. She works five, sometimes six days a week. How much does your new pastor work? One, maybe two days a week? Come on, man! You think that's fair? You think that's right?"

Jim's mind was racing. Malik was undeterred. "So, Grandma hits some hard times for real, right? Gotta take care of her four grandbabies on ten bucks an hour. And so a few folks—who don't even know her, mind you—say, 'Let's start bringing her a box of groceries once a week. I bet that'll make her happy. I bet that'll help for real.'" Malik realized he was laying it on thick. He decided to pause for a moment.

Jim had learned in the courtroom that anger was one emotion he could not afford to get the best of him. Malik was obviously passionate about this, and he knew there were few statements he could make at the moment to douse the flames. So he scratched his chin for a second and then chose his words carefully.

"You're right, Malik. Thirty-six years is a long time. Let me ask you something. Did your grandma ever ask for a raise? I mean, did she ever share her struggles or remind her supervisors that she's been there as long as she has?"

"Yeah," Malik replied. "Twice. Years ago she said she

asked for a raise. The church told her there wasn't any money for something like that. But at that same time they were doin', like, a big ol' expansion for their youth group building or somethin'. She just wanted a few measly dollars more an hour.

"The second time she was told no too. Same answer. 'There ain't no money.' But again, they were rollin' out a new retirement plan for church staff. Most of them hadn't even been there for more than five years. She didn't get offered the retirement benefit or a raise, but she got the privilege of cleaning up the trash after the staff party where they announced the benefit. My grandmother has been workin' there since she was almost sixteen. But it looks like she's gonna be there until she's seventy because she's got no retirement. No way to step away. So, your church thinks they're givin' us some help, but really? You're just keeping us in a ditch and throwin' us some blankets."

"Okay," Jim responded. "But then why didn't she just find another job? If she doesn't like the pay, then why not just move on?"

"Work where, man?" Malik responded with raised eyebrows. "There ain't no good jobs in Edgewood. All the jobs that pay anything are over on your side of town. When my granddad split, my grandma had to drop out of college to take care of her kids. She left them with her mom, worked, and came home. She never went back to school. A woman her age with no education ain't gonna get a better job for real. That's just how it is."

Jim opened his mouth to offer some commentary about Malik's granddad leaving the house, but he thought better of it. Malik eased his feet closer to the hearth to warm his toes. The momentary silence was refreshing. But Malik wasn't finished.

"I just don't understand why she doesn't matter to y'all." Malik gazed hard into the flames. "I mean, thirty-six years is like a legacy, man, and almost nobody there even knows her name. Your pastor can go out of town and see the world for a month if he wants, right? They call it a sabbatical or something like that. My grandma got real sick one time, and y'all almost fired her after she was gone for more than a week. I just don't get that kinda stuff. Does she matter? Your pastor still calls her Wanda. That ain't her name, and she's old enough to be his mama, but he calls her Wanda! And she still has to call him 'Pastor Jones.' He could give the sorriest sermon on Sunday and people wouldn't care for real, but if my grandma ever left the church bathroom a mess before the service, then she'd pry be gone."

Jim stared at Malik. The vacant look on the young man's face caused him to wonder if Malik was just talking to himself at this point.

Jim glanced at his watch. It was almost 10:45. He wondered if help would ever come. He shuddered slightly and for a moment wished he had a blanket.

12

THE FEAR

10:45 p.m., Monday before Thanksgiving

THE CONVERSATION REACHED AN AWKWARD LULL.
The crackling fire and the groan of the cabin under the
lashing winds were the only noises. For the time being they
were warm enough. But they were still stuck together, each
with his own thoughts.

Jim thought back to when he had been trapped in an
elevator. He was barely thirteen years old. He could hear
voices above him and knew that it was just a matter of time
before someone heard the alarm and his yelling and came
to help him. This was different. No one was around—even
if they were, if he stepped outside, the raging wind would
throw his voice back down his throat the moment he opened
his mouth. His phone was gone; Malik's was dead. Compared
to this, Jim would relish being stuck in an elevator again.

Malik didn't mind the silence. In his tiny house with three younger siblings and the blaring television, silence was a rare and wonderful gift. Many nights he was woken by blaring sirens roaring down the streets or by shouting in a neighboring apartment. Other times it was the *pop-pop-pop* of gunfire somewhere down the block. Rare moments of silence afforded him an opportunity to read and to think.

He hadn't intended to get so loud and defensive with Jim earlier. Ordinarily he was more respectful around adults, and he almost always felt a particular kind of awkwardness around affluent white people like Jim. His own brashness had surprised him. But his discovery of Jim's mission of charity in his community roused some monstrous emotions in him. The strong words of his Uncle Keith came to his mind.

A fool will argue over almost anything, Malik. Don't be a fool. But a good man will never run from a good argument. Not from anyone or for any reason. With that stuff between your two ears, the Lord gave you good sense to fight and win a good argument. He also gave you those two fists you have to fight a good fight—but only if the stuff between your ears isn't enough.

Largely because of his uncle's influence, Malik had thrown himself into a variety of good arguments. And as far he knew, he'd won them all. For other reasons he had thrown himself into his own fair share of good fistfights as well.

When Malik was younger, he spent three straight summers living with Uncle Keith. As a budding teenager, he found those summers to be as formative and invigorating as any time in his life.

After nearly ten minutes of silence, Jim finally released a loud sigh, closed his eyes, and let his chin fall on his chest. Malik looked over at him and studied his troubled face.

"You scared, Jim?" Malik asked softly.

"Scared of what?" Jim asked, his eyes still closed.

"Scared that we're gonna die out here tonight."

Jim wiggled his clenched jaw back and forth a few times before speaking. "I've been scared all night, Malik. Scared to drop off the food in your neighborhood. Scared to go in your apartment complex. Scared to buy gas at that station. Scared when I saw you and those other thugs running toward me. Scared when you jumped in my car with your gun. I've been scared driving into nowhere on a freezing cold night with no food, no phone, no fuel, and no plan. And now that we're stuck here in this cabin and there's probably no help around for miles, I'm still scared. I have no clue what's going to happen to me." He opened his eyes and looked at Malik. "Are you scared?"

Malik gave a slight shrug. "Yeah. A little, I guess. So you were afraid to come into my neighborhood, man?"

Jim laughed. "Are you really asking me that right now? The whole reason my wife didn't want me coming to Edgewood is because of *exactly* what happened. She didn't want me to get mugged or carjacked. It wouldn't have been a big surprise if maybe one of those things happened, right? But I got the double whammy tonight, didn't I?"

"Man! It ain't always like that for real!" Malik replied. "Those three clowns in the store were gonna mess me up. I was in that store to buy my grandma some groceries, not to rob nobody or jack your car. That was outside of my control. Besides, I bet you drive down to Edgewood 364 other nights out of the year and nothing close to those things happens. You might have some dude come up to you and try to bum some change or offer you a taste, but gettin' robbed and your car stolen—nah, chances of that happenin' again are like zero, man."

"Yeah?" Jim replied. "Well, it did happen, didn't it? The main reason people from my neighborhood don't come to Edgewood is because they're scared to death of something like this happening. And what you and those punks at the gas station did tonight isn't going to help a whole lot, is it? You didn't really help change the statistics."

Malik's brow furrowed. "Quit saying 'people from my neighborhood' and just say it like it is: 'white people.' White people don't like coming to my neighborhood. White people are scared of Edgewood. Scared of thugs, pimps, drug dealers, and hoes, right? I'm guessin' you saw one of those on every corner, didn't you? Everywhere you looked, right? Because that's what people from *my* neighborhood are . . ."

Jim shook his head. "It isn't just white folks from Stone Brook who are scared to come to Edgewood. I have two black friends in my law firm. Neither of them would set

foot in your neighborhood without some serious concerns—
some serious fear. I've heard them talk about Edgewood and
this side of town, and they aren't fans."

Malik paused. "Did it ever occur to you that people
from my neighborhood are scared about rollin' up in your
neighborhood?"

"Whatever," Jim replied. "When's the last time someone
has had their head bashed in by some thugs in Stone
Brook? When's the last time someone had their car stolen
at gunpoint when they were filling up their tank?"

"Robbery and thugs ain't the only things to fear. There
are other things people like me gotta worry about. Stuff you
wouldn't understand."

"Oh yeah? Like what?" Jim leaned back, as Malik leaned
forward. This would be a hard story to tell—and just as hard
for Jim to hear.

■ ■ ■

*Malik wiped the sweat from his forehead. The September sun
hung high in the afternoon sky. The grass in his yard was golden
and brittle after three straight weeks without rain. He kicked a
clod of it and unearthed a small cloud of gray dust. It twisted
around his shoes in the light breeze.*

*He squinted and put his hands over his eyes, hoping to see
Uncle Keith's car come around the corner. His uncle was always
on time; that's why Malik came outside ten minutes early. He
didn't want to miss his opportunity to spend time with the man.*

He squatted down and picked up a stone, rolling it around

in his palm as he whistled awkwardly. Just then he heard a honk. He smiled as he saw his uncle approaching in his old brown Mercedes.

Malik raced toward the car, waving his hands. Uncle Keith flashed him a big grin and pulled up alongside the curb. His car was old but meticulously clean and shiny. Malik opened the passenger door and jumped inside. Uncle Keith placed his powerful hand on his nephew's shoulder.

"You ready to roll out of here and get your grandma?" Uncle Keith asked in his low and gravelly voice.

"Yessir," Malik said. He latched his seat belt and wiggled comfortably into the weatherworn leather seat.

"Well, let's do it then."

Uncle Keith came around a lot. He was large and handsome with a clean-shaven head and a well-groomed goatee. He had recently accepted a professorship at a college out of town, but he made it his habit to regularly drive back home and check in on his sister and her two kids. His backseat was almost always filled with boxes of books and manila folders stuffed with papers. His dark brown satchel, containing his laptop and lecture notes, was situated on the floorboard behind his seat. As a man who had served in the Marines for ten years, he carried himself with great dignity. He was a man the block respected, the prize of the Thompson family.

"So, you want a chance at five dollars?" Uncle Keith said as he elbowed his nephew.

"Oh yessir!" Malik chirped. He loved it when his uncle played one of his trivia games.

"Now, how old are you?"

"C'mon, Uncle Keith!" Malik said with a laugh. "You know I'm eight years old."

"Eight. Eight." Keith slapped his forehead with the palm of his hand. "I just keep forgetting how you're growing up."

They pulled up to a traffic light. Keith forgot about his game with his nephew for a moment as he watched two young men arguing and fussing about ten feet from the vehicle. Malik could hear their profanity through the closed window. One of the kids was shirtless and covered in tattoos. Both of them had pants sagging six inches below their waists. Keith just shook his head.

"Don't end up like those two knuckleheads right there, son," Uncle Keith said sternly as he gripped the steering wheel. "Because where are those two boys going?"

"Going nowhere, sir."

"That's right," Keith said proudly. "Going nowhere."

"I still want to get those five dollars," Malik prodded. "Don't forget."

Uncle Keith smiled as the light turned green. They moved up the ramp and onto the interstate. "Okay. Okay. Five dollars if you can answer five questions. How's that sound? It's all or nothing."

Malik nodded. Uncle Keith snapped his fingers twice. "All right. For starters let's do a little geography—yeah, that sounds good. You tell me, Mr. Malik, what's the capital of the United States of America?"

Malik grinned. "Ah that's easy, Uncle Keith. Washington, D.C. I'm gonna take all your money if you keep giving me questions like that."

"No sir. The first question is always an easy one. Question number two. It's a spelling question. Spell for me the word 'ridiculous.'"

Malik closed one eye and gathered his thoughts. "Ridiculous. R. I. Umm. D. I?"

"Is that a question?" Uncle Keith asked. "Because there will be no lifelines here, sir!"

"No! No!" Malik said, waving his hands. "R. I. D. I. C. U. L. Uhhhh. O? U . . . S! Ridiculous!"

"Whoa! Uh-oh! Malik Thompson is two for two, baby. But can he keep up under the pressure?" Keith gave Malik a playful shove.

"Bring it on! I'm ready!" Malik shouted. "Those five bucks are gonna be all mine!" Malik cherished these moments with Uncle Keith. He loved how effortlessly and freely he wove his car in and around the other vehicles. He felt like they were racecars. No one could pass them, and no one could stop them.

"Well, you know," Keith said warily, "no trivia game can exist without at least one good math question, right?" Malik's eyes widened slightly, and then he frowned. Uncle Keith held his finger in the air. "But remember. The questions only get harder. So, do you want to have that math question now or save it until last?"

Malik sighed. "I'm not too good at math. Might as well give it to me now and try to get it over with."

"That's not the attitude of a winner there," his uncle chided him. "You need to believe. I didn't become a college professor hitting a bunch of softballs. No sir. Every now and then you need to step up to the plate and take on a real challenge."

Malik nodded. "Okay. Give it to me then."

"If your mama pays you $1.25 every day to do the dishes, how much money will you have after seven days?" Uncle Keith shot a quick glance at Malik. A slight smile furled at the edge of his mouth.

"Man! I wish Mama would pay me to do the dishes."

"Hush, boy! Don't let this math question put any nonsense in your head."

Malik put both hands on his lap and started tallying the amount with his fingers. "Whoa!" Keith said, shaking his head. "Put those things away, son. No sir. I said no lifelines."

"Ah c'mon! I can't add without using my fingers. You gotta let me. Please!"

"No sir," Keith said firmly. "Use what the good Lord put between your ears. Fingers or no fingers, a man has got to be able to do some basic math."

Malik sighed and threw himself back in the seat, but he straightened himself quickly when he saw his uncle's disapproving stare. His shoulders sank slightly, and he gazed glumly out the window. The landscape had changed drastically. The throb and grind of the city were behind them. There were no more little homes, abandoned strip malls, or battered brick buildings. Here there were far more trees shrouding large houses nestled comfortably in rolling hills. Most of the cars were passing them now. Uncle Keith had both hands on the wheel. It appeared that his carefree spirit had fallen away somewhere a few miles back on the interstate.

"Come on, Malik," his uncle said. "You can't have all day. Fifteen more seconds and I need your answer."

"Uh. Okay. Ummm." Malik had numbers swirling in his head. He couldn't organize them the way he wanted. He ached to use his fingers.

"Five seconds."

"Eight dollars and twenty-five cents." Malik spouted the answer with desperation.

His uncle frowned and shook his head. "No. Come on, son. Think about it. It's not that hard."

"I told you," Malik retorted. "I can't count without my fingers. I just can't."

"Well. It looks like my five dollars are safe for another week or two. If only you hadn't given up and shut down, you might have just given your brain a chance to solve the problem."

"Ah come on!" Malik pleaded, even though he knew his uncle wouldn't change his mind. "Give me another problem. Give me another chance. I'll get it this time."

Uncle Keith turned on his signal and got off the interstate. They merged onto a spacious two-lane road. Malik loved this part of the drive. The houses in the neighborhood were large. The yards were lush with green grass and ornate bushes. Malik liked to imagine what it would be like to wake up in the morning in one of those gigantic houses. He envisioned his mom fixing him a hot breakfast in her big kitchen before he went outside to play under the shade of the large oak trees. He could imagine riding his bike down the sidewalk and waving to folks walking their dogs and jogging. There were no burned-out homes or houses that were boarded shut. No one's grass was waist high. There was no trash along the curbs or angry *graffiti spattered on the walls. He always felt a little more at peace here.*

But Uncle Keith's behavior was different. He was constantly checking his mirrors. At every red light, he'd always pause an extra second before accelerating once the light turned green again. This was curious to his young nephew.

"Did you tell Grandma we were coming this time?" Malik asked.

"Yes. She's expecting us in the next couple of minutes." Uncle Keith shot a glance at the clock on the dash. Just ahead was the bus stop where Malik's grandmother waited each afternoon. Sitting on the bench, waiting for the bus, were two older African American women and a Hispanic man wearing a hard hat and eating a sandwich. Malik watched them as Uncle Keith drove by. He pictured his grandmother getting dropped there each morning at 8:00 a.m. and then getting picked up again in the evening. This was her routine. He was glad they could pick her up today.

Mars Chapel was just eight blocks ahead. Malik could see its elongated steeple looming above the trees in the distance, the white cross rising prominently in the sky against a rolling back- drop of fluffy clouds.

Just then, Uncle Keith let out a slight sigh and took a long glance in the rearview mirror. Malik looked at his uncle and then slowly turned to look over his shoulder. He spotted the white and black police car behind them. It was riding close to their rear bumper. Malik glanced back at Uncle Keith, who continued to grip the steering wheel with both hands and shoot frequent glances into the mirror.

"Come on," Uncle Keith said under his breath. "Just move on by, friends."

They drove almost six blocks this way. Uncle Keith even slowed down a little bit, but the police car continued to tail him.

The light ahead turned yellow. They had plenty of time to make it through the intersection before the light turned red. But Uncle Keith hit the brakes. They decelerated rapidly.

Malik looked curiously at his uncle's agitated face. "You okay?" he asked.

"I'm fine, son." Uncle Keith turned to his nephew and offered a wink.

They waited for the light to change, and Uncle Keith turned on his signal. He tapped his ring finger on the steering wheel and stared straight ahead. Malik wanted to take one more look behind them but decided not to. The light turned green, and they slowly took their right-hand turn onto the road that headed up to the church. The squad car took the turn as well. Uncle Keith frowned.

Just ahead was a gas station. The speed limit sign said 15 mph; they were about to enter a residential area. Just then they heard the shrill chirp from the police car. The blue flashers on the roof of the squad car lit up. Uncle Keith mumbled something indiscernible under his breath and slowly pulled his car into the gas station parking lot.

Malik swallowed and turned his head just slightly to see if the police were following them. They were. His uncle pulled into the nearest open spot and put his car in park.

"*What do they want, Uncle Keith?*" Malik asked. "*You didn't do anything.*"

"*It's going to be fine, son.*" Keith's voice sounded calm—but his eyes betrayed something else.

The police car stopped in the center of the parking lot. Its lights flashed around off of the walls and gas pumps. Malik spotted the cashier inside the gas station as he leaned forward to see what was going on. A white woman stopped filling her van, hurriedly replaced the nozzle, and drove off.

The police did nothing for almost two minutes. Malik couldn't stand the mystery. "*What are they doing?*" he asked. "*Why are they just sitting there?*"

"*Tough to say,*" Uncle Keith replied. "*In a situation like this you just need to stay calm, son. We didn't do anything wrong. Just need to relax.*"

"*Yeah. But Grandma is going to start wondering where we are.*" Malik pointed at the clock on the dash.

"*Nothing we can do about that at the moment,*" Uncle Keith said, drawing a sharp breath through his nose and slowly exhaling it.

The doors on the police car opened. A squat and stout officer emerged from the driver side. He was young, and his hair was buzzed low on the sides. He had a finely trimmed red mustache and a pair of Ray-Bans affixed to his face. His partner exited the car on the passenger side. He was tall and gangly with a mop of strawberry-blond hair. He squinted awkwardly in the afternoon sun. Both of them approached the vehicle slowly.

Uncle Keith lowered his window as the stout officer

approached his side. He offered a cautious smile as the policeman came into view. "Afternoon, officer," he said kindly. "There
a problem?"

The officer flexed his jaw. "You got a taillight out."

Malik watched as the lanky officer rounded to the other side
of the car and looked at him through the window. He didn't like
the man's grim face—or the large black gun on his hip.

"Really?" Uncle Keith replied. "I didn't know that. I can get
that fixed right away. Thank you for letting me know."

"You work over here?" the officer queried gruffly.

"No," Uncle Keith answered calmly. "We're over here to get
my mother at the church up the road. I'm a professor over at—"

"Can I see your license and registration?" the policeman
interrupted in a monotone voice.

Malik leaned forward to take a better look at the man ques-
tioning his uncle. The church steeple in the distance appeared to
be growing out of the top of his head like a strange appendage.
The officer's face was taut and unflinching.

"No problem," Uncle Keith responded. He reached for his
glove box.

"Whoa! Easy there fellah." The officer placed his hand on his
gun and unclasped the holster.

"Huh? Oh, no," Uncle Keith said. "I need to get my registration from my glove box."

"Nice and slow, then," the policeman said, his eyebrows
tightened on his face. "Nice and slow."

Uncle Keith looked at the officer and then over at the glove
box. He reached his hand and slowly opened it up. The officer

kept his hand on his gun. Malik took another glance at the policeman outside of his window, and then back at the officer next to Keith. For a moment he imagined what a cat must feel like trapped between two angry dogs.

Uncle Keith pulled out an envelope and removed the registration papers before handing them to the policeman. "License?" the officer said flatly.

Uncle Keith shifted slightly in his seat and pulled out his wallet. He removed his driver's license and placed it in the officer's hand. "Like I was saying a moment ago, my nephew and I are driving to get my mother from work. She got off about five minutes ago, and she's waiting for us just up the hill. I can get the taillight fixed." Uncle Keith's words were calm but with an underlying tone of agitation.

The policeman relaxed his hand on his gun but said nothing. He spent a long time looking at the license and papers. He seemed to relish the awkward lull.

Malik was confused. He didn't understand why they couldn't just leave.

"What's in the back of the car here?" The officer outside Malik's door squatted down a little bit and looked at the items in the rear seat.

Uncle Keith replied, "I'm a professor at Harpers College. Those are my books, my papers, and my computer."

Two white teenagers in a blue BMW convertible rolled into the parking lot, blaring loud hip-hop music. One of them had an NY cap cocked sideways on his head. Both of the young men looked at the scene in front of them for a minute before jumping out of the car. One of them said something to the other, and they both burst out laughing before yanking open the door to the gas station and stepping inside.

"We're going to need you to step out of the vehicle," the short officer said.

"Why?" Uncle Keith replied defensively. "We've done nothing wrong. I can get that taillight fixed."

"Please step out of the car," the policeman said, tightening his jaw again. "Now."

"I don't understand," Uncle Keith retorted. "If you want to give me a ticket, then give me a ticket. But I don't need to get out of my car—that makes no sense!"

"Listen here." The officer placed his hand back on his gun. "You can step out of the car on your own, or we can snatch you out of the car. But we'd rather not do that in front of your boy here. Your choice."

Malik could feel the fear and the anger swirling in his stomach. He started to feel sick. Uncle Keith was such a big and respectable man, and these policemen were trying to make him feel so small. Malik's fists tightened in his lap as he waited to see what his uncle was going to do.

Uncle Keith gripped the steering wheel, closed his eyes, and took a few slow breaths through his nose. His head was bowed, and he sucked in his lips. He turned and looked at his nephew. Malik felt like he was peering into a deep well of pain and anger.

Finally, Uncle Keith relaxed his grip on the steering wheel. "I know my rights, officer," he said calmly. "A busted taillight *is not a reason for me to get out of my car. That's what you said this is all about. A busted taillight. You're abusing your power. You've given no reason for me to get out of my car. So give me one, because I know that a taillight ain't a reason for me to get out of my vehicle!" Uncle Keith stared hard into the officer's face.*

"John," the officer said snidely. "Looks like this one isn't going to cooperate. Go ahead and call in backup."

Uncle Keith shook his head and erupted into laughter. "Backup! Over a busted taillight? This is absolutely absurd!"

Officer John raised his radio to his lips but paused for a moment to see what Uncle Keith would do.

"Backup! Wow!" Uncle Keith said slowly. He reached for the door handle.

"Easy. Easy, fella." The officer opened the door and took one step back from the vehicle. "Keep your hands where we can see them."

"My name, officer, is Dr. Keith Thompson." Keith rose slowly from the car with his hands in the air. He towered nearly a foot and a half over the policeman.

"Spread your feet and put your hands on the vehicle."

Malik could no longer see his uncle's face, but he heard his two large hands come down on the roof of the car. He could see Uncle Keith's barrel chest rising and falling with each breath. Then he watched as the short officer started patting him down and slowly searching his pockets.

"Hey John," the officer said to his partner as he continued this search. "Go ahead and check the back of the vehicle."

"Now hold on! Hold on!" Uncle Keith bellowed over the roof. "I've done everything you've asked. What does this have to do with a broken taillight? You two are trampling all over my rights! This is totally ridiculous! You have no warrant— no motive for this!"

As Officer John reached for the back door and opened it, Uncle Keith took a slight step backward. The policeman behind him sprang into action, wedging Keith's arm behind him and driving him down hard on the hood of the car. Malik watched in horror through the front window as his uncle's torso came crashing hard in front of him. Uncle Keith's teeth were gritted and there was fire in his eyes. He wriggled and struggled for a moment but relaxed when he saw his nephew and the tears streaming down his face. The two locked eyes and just stared at each other.

Officer John was now behind Malik, rummaging loudly through the boxes in the back seat, tossing books on the floorboard and accidentally spilling one folder. Some of the papers fell out of the car and whisked down the pavement as the wind carried them away. The two young men from the convertible emerged from the store and stood on the sidewalk sipping large cups of soda as they watched the police. One had a half smile on his face. Malik wanted them to leave. When they finally got back in their car, their loud music erupted again, and they drove out of the parking lot.

Officer John gave up on the boxes and pulled out Uncle Keith's satchel. He placed it on the hood just opposite of Uncle Keith's head. He pulled out the laptop and a Moleskine notebook. He flipped through the notebook, frowned, and set it aside. In a side pocket he discovered a few pens and a clip containing Uncle Keith's business cards and his college ID badge. The policeman looked at the business cards and badge for a moment and then up at his partner.

"You need to look at this, Stuart." Officer John handed the cards and badge to his partner.

Officer Stuart still had Uncle Keith's arm behind his back, but with his free hand he took the ID badge. As he had done with the license and registration, he took an inordinate amount of time to look at them. Finally, he relaxed his grip.

"Okay. Okay. Easy there." He took a step back. "Looks like we had the wrong fella."

Uncle Keith righted himself and, with angry jerks of his hands, tried to straighten his disheveled shirt. He turned on his heels and faced Officer Stuart.

"The wrong fella, huh?" Uncle Keith said icily. "What does that mean?"

"You fit a description of a man we're looking for, sir." Officer John scratched his nose for a moment.

"A description?" Uncle Keith asked angrily. "Care to explain?"

"Look," Officer Stuart said plainly, "you're free to go." He handed Uncle Keith his ID, license, and registration. "Just be sure to get that taillight fixed soon."

"No, sir!" Uncle Keith retorted loudly. "It's not that simple. I need an explanation for all this nonsense!"

"And I said you're free to go," Officer Stuart said. "No ticket this time. Just grab your mama and go home. Come on, John."

The two policemen walked back to their car and got inside. They cut off the swirling blue lights, drove slowly around the parking lot, and circled back out the way from which they had come. Uncle Keith just stood there with a clenched jaw as they drove out of view. His shoulders were heaving. Malik sat in silence as his uncle struggled to regain his composure.

An entire minute passed before Uncle Keith walked slowly around the parking lot to try to retrieve his scattered papers. Malik reached for his door handle to help but then decided to stay where he was. He watched as his uncle stooped to retrieve a few sheets that were stuck in a puddle of oil and grime. Keith scrutinized them for a moment before angrily balling them up and tossing them into a nearby trash can. He threw his hands in the air, giving up on the pointless exercise, then slapped them on his legs before returning to the car.

Keith sat back in the driver's seat and slammed the door shut. He wiped his mouth with the back of his hand and looked at himself in the rearview mirror. Then he turned to his nephew.

"I'm sorry you had to see all of that, son. Are you okay?" He spoke softly, though the fire was still dancing around in his eyes.

Malik said nothing.

"I don't want you to tell your grandmother anything about this, you hear me?"

Malik wanted to speak, but he could only nod his head.

"I mean it, son," his uncle said. "Not a word."

With that he put the car in reverse and drove them out of the parking lot.

Jim looked at Malik as he finished his story. He didn't want to speak without thinking for a moment. Malik wanted Jim to say something. The standoff of silence was unsettling.

Finally Jim cleared his throat. "That's unfortunate," he said. "It's frustrating when the cops get the wrong guy."

Malik chuckled. "The wrong guy?"

"I mean, they obviously got your uncle confused with someone they were looking for, right?" Jim said, throwing his hands in the air. "I mean, that's awful when it happens, but they make mistakes."

Malik tightened his lips, shook his head, and sniffed.

"A mistake," he said coldly, "is something that happens once in a blue moon, man! That's just one story. My uncle got pulled over three more times that summer just going to pick up my grandma. I bet you he's been pulled over at least six to eight times on your side of town. And why? Because he 'looks like someone'? Come on, man! We both know it ain't that! It's just because he looks a certain way. Period."

Jim waited. He knew Malik wasn't done.

"My uncle is more educated and more decent than most of the folks who live over in your neighborhood. But when's the last time the cops rolled up on your ride or rolled up on one of your friends, huh? Probably never. Am I right? So yeah, we got reasons to be scared too. You think your neighborhood is like Disneyland or somethin', where everybody is safe and happy. I don't feel safe or happy over there.

In fact, now when I'm over there, I can't wait to get up and out of your neighborhood, man. Ask anybody where I live if they like it over where you live. Why do you think a lot of folks ride the bus? My uncle's experience ain't unique—happens all the time. In fact, if I'm drivin' your car through your neighborhood, I bet you I don't make it home without getting pulled over. Bet you!"

Jim grimaced. Silence resumed as the two stared back at the fire. Another gust of wind pried at the roof and quivered the walls. After a few moments Malik let out a soft chuckle. Jim turned slightly. "What's so funny?" he asked.

Malik shook his head. "It's cold, dark, and crazy out here, man. But I was just thinkin'. I bet we both feel safer out here right now than we do visiting each other's neighborhood. I don't know—that made me laugh."

Jim turned back and stared straight ahead as he wrestled with his thoughts. As strange as it sounded, Malik was right.

13

THE EDUCATION

11:45 p.m., Monday before Thanksgiving

JIM GOT UP TO THROW ANOTHER LOG ON THE FIRE. He glanced at his wristwatch. It was creeping toward midnight. Malik yawned and stretched his arms behind his head. "How long you think this stack will last?" he asked.

Jim plopped back in his chair and brushed some wood chips off his hands on his pant legs. He looked at the pile that was left and shrugged. "There's probably enough there to get us through the night and maybe a few hours into the morning. After that, it's tough to say. If these temps don't go back up, we'll have to brave the outdoors and hope there's some firewood around another cabin or something. I've never seen a storm or temperatures like this down here before in my life."

"I guess we could burn these chairs if we had to," Malik mumbled.

"Yeah, they'd buy another hour, maybe," Jim said.

Malik took another look at the pile of firewood and then back at the fire. "It's kinda funny, isn't it?"

Jim rolled his eyes. "What is?"

"I dunno. I've thought about dying a lot of times. I just never imagined that my hope for survival would hinge on a stack of firewood. Crazy, isn't it? I mean, you can literally watch hope disappear into smoke one log at a time. If things don't change, we're going to have to toss our last log—and then pray."

Jim stared at Malik for a moment. The young man sucked in his top lip and rubbed his hands in front of his face. "I've already been praying," Jim said.

"Yeah. For what?"

"I'm praying I can get out of here and get home."

"If we make it through this whole thing," Malik said, "everything turns out okay for you, man. I'm done no matter what happens. I can die of cold in this cabin, die once Mike and his boys get their hands on me, or die of loneliness in a cell block. One way or another, this does not end well for me."

"Sounds kind of hopeless to me."

"That's because it pretty much is hopeless, dude." Malik cut his eyes at Jim.

"Life doesn't have to be that way," Jim replied. "You made some bad choices. Bad choices come with consequences."

"Like what'cha mean?"

"Take tonight, for example." Jim stood up and rubbed his

shoulders with his hands. "You brought a gun with you to the grocery store. Who does that? Probably someone who's afraid of someone or something. But why is he afraid? When things got out of hand with your buddies in there, you fled. When a man runs from something, it always looks bad."

"So you gonna go all lawyer on me now?" Malik growled.

Jim ignored him and continued. "But why did things get out of hand in the first place? Those guys were mad at you about something. I'm guessing it wasn't random. I bet you did something specific that made them angry, right? Then you jumped in my car and used your weapon to coerce me into doing something I didn't want to do. Once we got on the road, you had no plan or strategy. You just said, 'Drive.' 'Where?' I asked you. You had no idea. So hours later we're trapped in a cabin in an ice storm—in a genuinely life-threatening situation. You made a series of bad decisions. And with those came some bad consequences."

"So you think it's that simple, huh?"

"Pretty much," Jim said. "Bad decisions are like dominoes. They tend to tip things over in ways that we don't want them to."

Malik smiled and nodded. "Let me ask you something."

"Shoot."

"Do you carry an insurance card?" Malik asked.

"Yeah. Why?"

"You tell me why," Malik retorted.

"In case I'm in an accident," Jim replied. "It's got me covered."

"Right," Malik agreed. "It's for those 'just-in-case situations,' correct? I mean, you don't pull it out unless it's really needed." Malik took the 9mm from the waistband of his pants and set it in his lap. "This is my insurance card, man. I don't have any intention of ever pulling it out. Like that card in your wallet, it stays hidden away for just-in-case scenarios. I've never pulled it on anybody—never robbed nobody—"

"Until tonight," Jim interrupted. "See? That doesn't work, Malik. I can't use my insurance card to hurt people or to rob them. It's protection *against* something happening. That's not how you used *your* insurance card tonight."

"Exactly. I pulled out my gun 'cause Mike and those dudes in the store just beat down my friend in the gas station and they were going to rough me up next. I carry my gun for guys like Mike and his squad. I don't know why I pulled it on you. That wasn't part of my plan. I saw you and your car, and, well, you were a lifeline, man. I had to get out of there. I just reacted."

Jim sat back down and crossed his legs. "Do you not get it, Malik? You carry a gun because Mike carries a gun. He carries a gun because so-and-so carries a gun. And it goes on and on and on. What if all of you just put your guns away and went to school? Or what if instead of robbing each other or selling drugs, you got a job?"

Malik clenched his teeth, but Jim wasn't finished. "You don't even make any sense. Earlier tonight you told me that white people have this unreasonable fear of your neighborhood and that what happened to me tonight was an anomaly. And yet you carry a gun around with you because you don't want those types of things to happen to you. Which one is it? No kid carries a gun in the back of his pants unless he's afraid that everyone else has a gun stuffed down the back of their pants. Either that, or he plans to use that gun to take something or do something to someone who doesn't have a gun."

"I feel you," Malik acknowledged. "But what I said was that you, a white dude visiting my neighborhood for thirty minutes to drop off some hummus and shoot some pictures, had little to fear. I didn't say you'd have nothing to fear if you moved next door to me. But, man, you make it all sound so simple: Go to school. Get a job. You're an idiot if you think you understand my life—"

"Here we go!" Jim slapped his legs and stood up again. "Let me guess. You're a victim, right? The poor black kid with no dad and no options. Raised on Tupac. No good schools. Poverty. Blah blah blah. Cut out the excuses, kid! Your life probably has had some challenges that mine hasn't. But at the end of the day, we all make choices. I have a hard time finding sympathy for people who continue to make bad ones and don't own up to it—or who just keep making excuses. Your grandmother has a job, doesn't she? Does she carry a gun to Mars each day? I doubt it. Why don't you follow her example instead of being a thug and expecting people to feel sorry for you?"

"So I'm guessing you made all the good choices along the way, right?" Malik blurted out.

"I worked hard. I went to school. I studied. I respected the law. I went to college, then to grad school. I worked tons of different jobs from the day I was fifteen years old. I didn't do everything perfect, but I made a lot of good choices, and it got me somewhere." Jim stretched his arms and rested his hands on his head. "That's how life works."

"You made those choices because they were easy," Malik replied.

"Excuse me?" Jim said, his lips tightening.

"You wouldn't last a day at my school, Jim."

"And here we go again!" Jim said, throwing his hands up in the air.

"I won't bore you, man. But let me tell you a story."

■　■　■

Ms. Jones leaned back from staring at her computer screen and barked at the class. "Everyone in here needs to sit down, shut up, and just watch the movie! If you keep on hollering, I'll turn it off and hand out some homework."

Malik sighed. He hated his chemistry class, and he hated Ms. Jones even more. It was Tuesday. They were watching The Fast and the Furious 3 *for the second time this quarter. Most of his classmates were standing and talking. Aside from the periodic table on the wall and a poster of a kitten holding a test tube, there wasn't any evidence of chemistry in the entire class-room. It had been this way for the last eighteen weeks.*

Ms. Tuck, the usual chemistry teacher, was still out on medical leave after trying to break up a fight in the gym.

Ms. Jones was an old, tenured teacher who did nothing but show videos and scream vain threats at the kids. No one cared or responded.

Malik sat in the back with his history book open. Mr. Dukes, his history teacher, was the only instructor who attempted to teach each day. His class was the only one that Malik actually enjoyed.

Just then the door opened. The assistant principal, Dr. Griffin, walked in with a clipboard in his hand. He gave Ms. Jones a quick glance, but she never looked up from what she was watching on her computer. A few of the students noticed him in the door and sat down, but the majority of the class continued to talk, laugh, and play with their phones.

"I need everyone's attention!" Dr. Griffin shouted over the din. He glared at the class through his glasses. "Sit your butts down and give me your attention!"

"Docta Griff!" one of the kids, William, hollered from the back. "What up, Docta Griff!"

The assistant principal frowned. "Ah, Mr. Will, good morning, sir. Thank you for your greeting. I need you to head to the office."

William frowned and cocked his head backward. "The office? What'd I do?"

Dr. Griffin turned to Ms. Jones. "Would you please turn off that TV? I can't hear myself think."

Ms. Jones picked up the remote and clicked off the television without looking up from her computer. Dr. Griffin looked back at his clipboard. "Let's see . . . Jamal Anderson, Shaquita Bird,

John Cole, Everson Masterson, Tyrone Smith, Mike Thomas, William Thompkins . . . and . . . Brenden Watson. Please grab your things and head to the office."

Brenden turned to Malik. "Man, what the—? They sending me home, bro?"

Malik glanced at his friend and rubbed his chin. He watched as the dismissed classmates started to shout and curse in dismay.

"Standardized testing starts tomorrow, doesn't it?" Malik said.

"Yeah, I think so. So what?"

"My guess is they're tryin' to boost the stats, dude," Malik said with a slight shrug.

"Huh?"

"Look at the list, bro," Malik said, shaking his head. "Jamal is failing like every single class. Shaquita can hardly read. Tyrone and William don't even try—they go to sleep during testing like every year." Malik offered Brenden a knowing smile. "You do too, bro. They want to boost the numbers and get out from being a failin' school."

"So they're gonna suspend us?" Brenden said. "That ain't right!"

Dr. Griffin was a large man and able to shout over the disgruntled classroom. "I don't need to repeat myself again! If I called your name, grab your stuff and head to the office. Now!"

"What'd we do wrong, Dr. Griff?" Jamal shouted as he balled up his fists. Several of the kids turned their heads toward the door as a small pack of loud students moved down the hallway toward the office.

"Yep," Malik said. "That's what they're doin'. I just saw

*Patrick and Cameron. Central did somethin' like this last year.
Remember? They sent like thirty kids home for three or four
days." He shook his head. "This is ridiculous, bro."*

*Brenden looked at Malik in disbelief and then turned to Dr.
Griffin. "You sending us home because you think we're stupid?"*

*Dr. Griffin flinched slightly before speaking. "Mr.
Brenden, it's time to go. Grab your things now. You and the
others I just called are excused from taking the tests this week.
You're making a bigger deal out of this than it needs to be. If
anyone continues to argue with me, you'll be going home for a
long time."*

*Jamal stood up with a grin on his face. "Aye! Dr. Griff said
we don't have to take that test. That thing is too boring, man!
I'm cool with that. Let's go, y'all."*

*Brenden looked at Malik. "You should go, dude," Malik
said. "This is lame, but there's no reason to make things worse.
Just treat it like vacation or somethin'."*

*Brenden sniffed and nodded. "Cool, bro. You go ahead
and take the test then. Boost the stats for us, or whatever." He
snatched his backpack off the floor and headed toward the door
with his classmates. Dr. Griffin pushed his glasses up his nose
and watched Brenden as he exited. He took another look at
Ms. Jones, but she was still engrossed with her computer.*

■　■　■

"So they just sent those kids home?" Jim interrupted. "For
what? Didn't the parents care? I'm guessing they didn't stand
for having them sent home for no reason."

"I don't know if the parents cared," Malik replied. "The administration had some old disciplinary stuff on almost every kid they sent home: fighting, defiance in the class-room, cheating, some other nonsense that they held on to until this week of testing. They had a 'reason' for why each kid was sent home. Not *everyone* knew why *those* kids were told to leave that week. Some just thought the school was handing out a bunch of suspensions. But some of us knew. They sent over forty kids home tryin' to get our stats over the line so that we wouldn't be a failin' school no more."

"Did it work?" Jim asked.

"Huh!" Malik laughed. "They tried to make it work."

■ ■ ■

Dr. Griffin walked over to Ms. Jones's desk and handed her a blue folder. Then he walked out the door. Ms. Jones took another minute to finish what she was watching on her computer screen before clicking it off and standing up.

"All right class, listen up!" Many of the students continued to discuss what had just happened with their classmates. "Tomorrow we start the standardized testing. These tests are very important for our school." She grabbed the folder off the desk and started walking down the aisles, handing each student a stapled packet.

"Is this another crossword puzzle?" Briana commented from the front of the class. Ms. Jones ignored her.

Malik took his packet and studied it for a minute. "Yo," Benny said as he turned to Malik. "Is this some kinda review sheet? Aye, Ms. Jones. What is this? You can't be givin' us a science test because we haven't learned any science in here all year."

Several students laughed. Others nodded their head in agreement. Ms. Jones stood in the front of the class and smacked the folder with her hand. "This," she said loudly, "is the answers to the science section of the standardized test."

"So you're just givin' us the answers?" Benny asked, incredulous.

"We're going to spend the next forty minutes studying this together." Ms. Jones pulled out a packet. "Let's get busy."

Malik looked around the room. There were a few surprised faces. A couple of his classmates shrugged, but within thirty seconds everyone was quiet and absorbing the answers on the sheet of paper. He sighed and joined the crowd.

■ ■ ■

"What they did is illegal," Jim said.

"Yeah, probably," Malik said. "But you think anyone cares? Do you care? Who cares about what happens at Edgewood High, man? Nobody for real. Our stats don't matter to nobody."

Jim turned back toward the fire to think for a moment. Malik chuckled and shook his head. "It didn't make a difference. They sent like the bottom ten percent of our class home along with most of the troublemakers. Then they gave out the study guides for science to everybody. Almost everyone crushed that section on the test. But only a handful of us did okay on the rest of it. Most of the smart kids there don't care enough to pull that school out of the hole it's in. We stayed a failing school."

"That's ridiculous!" Jim said. "I mean, cheating went on at my school. But it was usually a handful of kids with their own elaborate schemes. I've never heard of anything that drastic before."

"So does Edgewood sound like a place where you'd be able to work hard, study, focus, and make all your 'good choices'?"

Jim remained silent, so Malik continued. "I've been going there for four years. I can count on one hand how many teachers actually care enough to teach each day. Most of 'em are old and tenured and don't care. I can count on two hands and about six of my toes how many times the police have been up there and pulled guns and knives off of my class-mates. I lost track of how many fights I've seen 'cause there are probably two to three good ones each week. So, when you make it sound so simple, like 'Hey, just go to class, just pay attention, just do your work, make good choices, blah, blah, blah'—you lose me, man. My guess is that your tough-est choices each day were which girl to ask out or what to eat for lunch in the cafeteria."

One of the large, glowing logs at the base of the fire was permeated with jagged fissures of orange. The heat pulsated in it as if the log were breathing. With a sharp crack it disintegrated into several coals. Jim watched in silence, then jumped up and tossed in another log, unleashing a cloud of sparks that swirled around and up the chimney like fireflies.

14

THE CONFUSION

12:25 a.m., Tuesday before Thanksgiving

MALIK COULD FEEL SLEEP CLOUDING HIS MIND
and tugging at his eyelids. The waves of heat from the fire
comforted him, and the dancing flames mesmerized him
into a trance. But his back hurt, and the hard chair was
uncomfortable. He groaned and stood up. Jim was battling
his own weariness, and Malik's movement startled him. He
lurched slightly.

"Dang, man," Malik said. "I think my butt fell asleep." He
rubbed his rear end. "I can't feel nothin' back there right now."

Jim dragged his hands wearily across his face as Malik
jogged in place for a minute to revive his legs.

"I'm hungry," Jim said. He held his hands to his stomach.

"Me too," Malik replied. He feigned a few punches at
the shadows.

"My wife was cooking her famous chicken casserole tonight," Jim continued, wistfully. "I bet she would have even let me sample a piece of the apple pie she was saving for Thanksgiving."

"You know what I could go for right now?" Malik flopped back in his chair.

Jim was still dreaming of the apple pie, topped with some vanilla ice cream. "What's that?"

"A deep-dish pizza, man," Malik said, wide-eyed. "Pepperoni. Yeah . . . deep dish pepperoni from Pizza Hut."

"If I had my phone," Jim mumbled, "or if yours still worked, we could probably get one delivered."

"Psh! Pizza Hut would probably deliver way out here in the middle of this hunting camp before they ever delivered a pizza to my apartment."

"You don't have Pizza Hut in Edgewood?" Jim asked, with surprise in his voice.

"We got one," Malik said. "But they don't deliver no more. Nobody delivers in Edgewood for real."

"Why's that?"

"Too many delivery dudes were gettin' jumped and robbed." Malik suddenly realized he was validating Jim's fears of his neighborhood even more. "So one by one they stopped delivering."

"Mugging the pizza guy," Jim said. "Now you're starting to understand—"

"I know what you're gonna say, so don't say it."

Jim frowned. "I'm just saying, once the pizza guy doesn't

feel safe in a neighborhood, there isn't much hope that anyone will. It makes absolutely no sense whatsoever to rob and hurt someone like that—it makes even less sense when people rob and hurt the very folks who are trying to help them."

"What's that supposed to mean?" Malik asked.

■   ■   ■

Jim raced down the hallway dodging nurses and orderlies in his way. The ER was the last place he expected to be that morning, but when he heard about his old college roommate, he came straight to the hospital.

The storm from the night before had knocked almost a third of the city's power out. Several homes, including his, were still waiting for the electricity to be restored. The power company was out in force, cutting limbs and fixing lines.

Jim paused in front of Sam's room and knocked three times before pushing the door open. As he entered the room, he saw Sam's girlfriend, Ginny, and his mother sitting down and talking softly. "Jim," Ginny said with a weak smile. She wiped a strand of hair out of her face and offered him a hug.

Jim nodded at Sam's mother. "Good morning, Ms. Langston. How are you both doing?"

"We're making it," Ginny replied. She placed her hand on Ms. Langston's knee.

Jim turned toward his friend in the bed. "How's my boy Sam doing?" What he saw took him aback. The left side of Sam's face was purple and swollen. There were stitches below his eye. He wore a neck brace. Dried blood was caked in one of his eyebrows and in his hair. His lips were split in two places. He was sleeping.

"What happened?" Jim asked, turning back to the two women. "I know those storms were awful last night. Did he fall from the truck? Or did something fall on him? He looks terrible."

Ms. Langston shook her head. "He got mugged, Jim," Ginny said. A few tears formed in her eyes.

"Mugged?" Jim asked, incredulous. "I don't get it. Wasn't he out restoring power last night?"

"His crew services the west side," Ms. Langston said softly. "He was in the truck while his partner was in the lift repairing a line."

Jim narrowed his eyebrows.

"Some men came up to the truck," Ms. Langston continued, "and told him to give them his wallet. He told them he didn't have any money—you know Sam . . ."

"He never has any cash with him," Jim said, shaking his head.

"One of the guys hit him in the face," Ms. Langston continued. "His friend in the lift saw the whole thing, but he couldn't do anything."

"I don't get it," Jim said. He was getting angry. "Wasn't he trying to get those people's power back on?" Ms. Langston nodded. "And they decided to rob and beat him in the middle of him trying to help them?"

"He handed them his wallet," Ms. Langston said with a sniff. "When they saw that he had no money, one of them

snatched him out of the truck. They beat him up and just left him there in a bloody heap."

"What types of animals do something like that?" Ginny asked with tormented eyes. "I mean, that's just inhumane." Jim was stunned.

"Some of his crew members have been mugged over there before," Ms. Langston said. "But nothing like this. He's been trying to transfer to working over on this side of town, but he's new to the company and has no pull."

Jim folded his arms. "Did they catch the guys who did this?" Ginny shook her head.

"Maybe those punks would think twice if they had to wait a month or two before they got their power turned on again," Jim muttered. "If they want to act like they're from the jungle, then they can live in the jungle. That makes me so mad!"

"Could you talk to Mary Beth's dad and try to get Sam transferred to another crew?" Ginny asked. "This is just too much."

"Sure, Ginny, I can talk to him. I think he'll listen."

"Please," Ms. Langston pleaded. "A mom can't stand to see her son like this. He's not a soldier or a policeman where he should have to be fearing for his life each day."

"It's dangerous enough just messing with power lines," Jim replied. "I'll do what I can to get Sam out of there."

■ ■ ■

Malik nodded. "Yeah, it's messed up when stuff like that happens. Makes me mad too."

"But what's the point? Do guys like that not realize that

they're acting no better than dogs—that they're giving that whole neighborhood a bad name? I've heard of people shooting at firemen before. That kind of stuff blows my mind. Can you explain it?"

Malik shook his head. "I really can't, man. I mean, I think a lot of people are just desperate. It's like some of them don't know what else to do."

"But my friend was there to turn on their power!" Jim said with exasperation in his voice. "He was there to help them—so they can watch their television, finish their laundry . . . iron their pants—whatever. Why do you rob and then beat a guy like that?"

Malik lowered his eyes and stared at the floor. But Jim was on a mission now. "When power guys come through our neighborhood, I wave and try to say, 'Thank you.' When it's hot outside I sometimes bring them a bottle of water. I appreciate them getting my neighborhood up and running again. Those guys are the good guys."

Malik slowly lifted his head and turned to Jim. "Like I said, I don't really have an answer for that mess, man. But I know that a lot of those dudes are truly . . . desperate."

"You keep saying 'desperate.' What's that supposed to mean? Does desperation give people the license to assault and rob people?"

"I ain't sayin' what those guys are doing is right. It's wrong, man. But you don't know what it's like to be in your twenties, with a criminal record, and no chance at a job—"

"But that gets back to what I said about choices!" Jim

interrupted. "If those guys are criminals, then they need to live with the consequences of their decisions."

"Consequences for life, man?" Malik shot back. "My cousin, Ricky, did a year in prison for selling some weed back when he was eighteen. He spent a year and a half in the pen. He did his time. He learned his lesson, right? He got out and looked for a job—a real job—almost every day for like six months. He's actually a really smart and talented dude. How many jobs do you think called him back for an interview after he checked the box that he was a felon?"

Jim just stared at Malik with his jaw set.

"Zero!" Malik continued. "Not one call. We're talking about places like Burger King, man. My cousin wasn't too proud and waiting for a specific kinda job. He just wanted a job. Period. I mean, how long would you keep lookin' for a job before you got desperate?

"You're married, right?" Malik was getting as worked up as Jim. "What would you do if absolutely nobody would hire you? I mean literally nobody. You sayin' you wouldn't hustle to feed your family . . . to stay alive? Look, I'm not sayin' that Ricky didn't make a mistake sellin' that dope, but should he pay the price for that for the rest of his life? He and his boys broke into a Radio Shack one night after it was closed. He didn't shoot or hurt nobody. A year and a half in prison is a consequence, man. But doesn't he deserve a second chance? They let him out, but he basically got the death sentence. Anybody could tell him no because of his past. He was completely jobless and eventually hopeless.

It's tough enough to find a good job just being black, but you put a felony record on top of that? You'd have a better chance getting a job with a turban on your head and a button on your chest that says 'I love the Taliban' than you would checking that box that says you're a felon! And that's messed up!"

"What's Ricky up to now?" Jim asked.

"He's locked up again," Malik said matter-of-factly. "A man has to eat. He gave up on the job hunt and started hustlin' again and got busted. He's serving another three years. One more offense and he's gone for good." Malik stopped for a minute and looked down at the floor. "But he's pretty much gone for good already."

Jim thought about Sam lying bruised and battered in the hospital bed. The same angry feelings stirred in him again. But he also thought about Ricky. What if Ricky and his friends had jumped Sam?

As if on cue, both of their stomachs growled at the same time. "Speakin' of being desperate," Malik said, breaking the tension, "I'm starvin'."

15

THE DAWN

7:02 a.m., Tuesday before Thanksgiving

THE NIGHT PROGRESSED IN SILENCE. Fatigue and
the warmth from the fire slowly overcame Jim and Malik,
driving them to a restless sleep. Now and then Jim woke
with a start and raced to resuscitate the dying fire. His
sudden movements startled Malik before he settled back into
a slumber. They repeated this process throughout the night
as it crept closer toward the dawn.

Eventually, Jim woke up and moved to the window. He
rubbed away the thin layer of ice on the glass with the sleeve of
his fleece. Sheets of snow rushed and swirled past him outside.

"Still bad out there?" Malik asked with a yawn.

"Yep," Jim said. He spun away from the window and
back toward his seat. "I'd say it might be getting worse. I've
honestly never seen anything like this."

Malik looked at the firewood. The stack was uncomfortably small. He started counting the remaining logs but quit because he knew the number would only discourage him more.

"So, what do you think they're sayin' out there?" Malik asked.

"Who?" Jim asked.

"Everybody," Malik said. "Haven't you been thinking about it on and off? I mean, you're like this big-time lawyer from Stone Brook. That has to make the news, right? People care about stuff like that. I bet it won't be long before they have the FBI lookin' for you."

Jim exhaled a slow breath and spoke glumly. "I keep thinking about my wife and what she's doing. She's probably just sitting downstairs on the couch right now, worried sick. That's what I keep thinking about."

"Yeah," Malik said softly. "Sometimes I think about my grandma and my brother and sisters. They gotta be worried too. But outside of them I doubt anyone cares a whole lot for real."

Jim frowned. "Come on. You have some friends, your mom, some other family. I bet they're worried too."

Malik gave a slight shrug. "Maybe. But I imagine that you disappearing has created some real interest. What was the name of that white girl from Stone Brook who disappeared, like six years ago? Ah man, I can picture her face. It was like Mindy . . . Mandy . . ."

"Mandy Swanson," Jim replied. "What about her?"

"I just remember that was on the news like every night for almost a year. I mean, 'Mandy Swanson, from Stone Brook, was with her college friends in Jamaica for their spring break,'" Malik said in his best news anchor voice. "She and her classmates were at a nightclub when she mysteriously vanished . . ."

"So what about it?" Jim interrupted. "That was a sad situation. My wife and a lot of people that I know were really upset about that. They never found her."

Malik offered up a wry smile. "I just remember her parents were on the news a bunch, crying and offering up money for information. They had like the FBI and CIA over there in Jamaica trying to find her, trying to find clues. It was a big deal. I mean, it was like a *reaaally* big deal. Everybody everywhere was talking about Mandy Swanson." He paused for a moment, then leaned forward and looked at Jim. "If this thing here gets dragged out much longer, won't be long until the whole country starts talkin' about you."

Jim's forehead furrowed into wrinkles. He glared back at Malik. "You think all of that with Mandy—all of this— is funny or something? People tend to get upset when people disappear. That's perfectly normal. It means they care!"

A corner of Malik's lips curled up into a smile. He weighed Jim's comment in his mind. "I guess that's what that means, maybe."

"What else could it mean?" Jim asked. He leaned back in his chair and folded his arms.

"Do you see it making the news if I don't reappear in

the next day or so?" Malik slowly turned his eyes to Jim. "Can you see someone on the news announcing, 'Malik Thompson, from Edgewood, has been missing for three days. His family last saw him heading to the Shop n' Snack at 5 p.m. to buy some milk and butter'?"

"Maybe," Jim said. "Probably."

"Come on man!" Malik said. "That ain't a story for real. And even if they did show it, most people would think, 'Ah. Edgewood. Yeah, he probably got merked or killed on his way home.' Then they'd change the channel or wait for the sports updates. But if they threw your face up on the screen, people would turn up the volume and they'd want to know more."

Jim shook his head, but Malik wasn't done. "I'm for real! When they show a black kid's face on the news most nights, what's it usually about? Come on, Jim. What's it about?" Jim lowered his eyebrows and stared into the darkness. Malik rapped Jim's knee with the back of his hand. "What's it about, Jim?"

Jim wasn't about to speak. He felt like he was being badgered on the witness stand. Malik waited a moment and sighed at his companion's silence. "Robberies. Murders. Drugs. Rape. Arrests. Dropping out of school. Right? That's why you see black boys like me on the news. Black boys disappearing ain't news, Jim. That's just what we do. But when Mandy Swanson from Stone Brook disappears, it's national news. Shoot! That news probably went global. Why? 'Cause rich white girls from Stone Brook don't disappear. *That* got everyone's attention."

Jim balled his fists up on the inside of his coat. Malik stared at him for a moment, waiting for him to speak, and then looked away.

Suddenly the cabin was illuminated with a faint pink glow. Malik jumped up from his chair so quickly that it fell over with a crash. He rushed to the window and rubbed away the icy film with his hand. A small, bright ball of fire glowed low in the sky behind a thick branch of pine needles.

With his nose just an inch from the glass, Malik could feel the cold outside. But he stood there with a smile and closed his eyes. He had never been happier to let the sun shine on his face.

16

THE DISCOVERY

7:33 a.m., Tuesday before Thanksgiving

THE SUNLIGHT SLOWLY FILLED THE CABIN, which was as welcome to Malik and Jim as a rescue chopper. As each minute passed, the shadows slowly eroded down the walls until they disappeared altogether. Jim was invigorated with hope. With the sun came the possibility of deliverance and being reunited with his wife. Inside the cabin, however, it was still tremendously cold. The heat from the fire dissipated not more than six feet from the fireplace.

Malik started to pace awkwardly in front of the fireplace. Jim watched him curiously. "What are you doing, Malik?" he finally asked. "Why are you walking around like that?"

"Maaaaaan," Malik said with a slight grimace. "I gotta use it!"

"Use what?" Jim asked, perplexed.

"You know, man . . . I'm in a tight, dude."

"In a tight?" Jim shook his head. "I'm lost, Malik. What's going on?"

Malik exhaled a long breath with his cheeks puffed out. "Come on, man. You know what I mean . . . I need to use the bathroom! I've been holding it for hours."

"Ohhhhh," Jim said perplexedly. "Why didn't you just say 'I need to use the restroom'? I'm guessing there's some kind of toilet in the back. If not, you can always go outside."

Malik stared at Jim, his head cocked to the side, his eyebrows raised. "You crazy?"

Jim shrugged. "You know what they say: 'There's nothing like peeing in the woods.'"

"Nobody I know says that! How long before Frosty the Snowman knocks on that door and asks if he can come inside and warm up? It's too cold," Malik mumbled. "I ain't peein' outside . . ." He walked quickly toward the back of the cabin.

In the light of day, the cabin was larger than they had realized. There was a small kitchen with a sink and a tiny gas stove. Some dilapidated wooden cabinets sagged precariously against the walls. In the far rear corner Malik discovered a door that he hoped was a restroom. He cautiously opened it and was relieved to see a small toilet. But then he looked up and frowned.

■　■　■

Jim was stirring the embers in the fireplace when Malik returned from the bathroom. Jim noticed the glum look on his face. "All better?" he asked.

"Yeah," Malik said. "It's just an old nasty hole in the ground pretty much."

"Better than nothing, I suppose," Jim replied. He threw one more log on the coal bed and stood up. "I think I might be in a tight too."

"If you need it, there's some Ku Klux Klan toilet paper hanging on the wall above the toilet," Malik said, slumping back in his chair.

"Huh? What do you mean?"

"You'll see."

A few moments later Jim returned to the fireplace and sat down next to Malik. "Not a big fan of the stars and bars, huh?"

Malik turned to Jim. "Is that what you call that redneck flag?"

Jim tightened his lips and nodded slightly. "You mean the Confederate flag. Some people call it the Stars and Bars."

"You a fan?" Malik asked.

Jim shrugged. "Not really. I mean, I don't hate it, but it's not like I have one flying in my front yard. My friends and I used to have Confederate-flag belt buckles and stuff back when we were in high school. A couple of guys had it on the back of their pickup trucks. I guess we thought they were cool."

"Yeah?" Malik said crossly. "Well, I hate it."

"Hate's a strong word," Jim replied.

"That's a flag for haters, man."

"Why's everything about race with you?" Jim said. "Not

135

everyone who has that symbol on their car—or in their bathroom, for that matter—hates black people. That's a pretty big stereotype."

"Wasn't that flag originally flyin' for people who were fightin' to keep slavery legal? Man, I studied the Civil War in school. Shoot! I wrote a whole paper on that flag for my history class."

"Not everyone who fought for the South in the Civil War owned slaves or were fighting to keep slavery legal," Jim protested. "The war was bigger than slavery. A lot of Confederate soldiers were fighting for other things that had nothing to do with it. Again, you're generalizing and stereotyping."

"Okay," Malik said. "But how many of the people who were marchin' behind that flag were fighting to *end* slavery?"

Jim rolled his eyes. "I think you're being too sensitive about the whole thing, Malik. I'm glad that slavery is over. That was an embarrassing and ugly part of our past. But there's more to that flag than just slavery. To a lot of good folks, it's part of their heritage—their heritage of standing up for their rights. It's a part of their history. Doesn't everyone's history have some good and some bad in it? A lot of the folks who fly that flag are remembering the good."

"I totally disagree, man. You're tryin' to make the whole thing sound complicated, but it's really pretty simple." Malik was calm but resolute. "When you see old footage of Klan rallies with black dudes swinging from trees by their necks, you always see that flag right there beside them. The white people who were throwin' rocks and cussin' at peaceful protestors during the Civil Rights Movement were toting that thing with them. It's a banner for hate and always has been.

"Have you ever seen a black person with a Confederate flag on their belt buckle or hangin' in their bathroom? You said some people are proud of it because it's part of their history or heritage or whatever? Well, it's part of black people's history too. And for us it's a symbol of hate and pain. The people who flew that flag and marched for it back in the day, whether it was the Civil War or the civil rights movement, felt a certain kinda way about black people. Whoever owns this place does too—I bet he'd flip if he knew a black kid just used his nasty bathroom . . ."

Jim exhaled a frustrated sigh. Malik continued. "My grandma says some folks from Mars have the flag on their cars—even one of the elders does. That doesn't sit right with me—I mean, I haven't read the whole Bible, but you think Jesus would wave that flag? Do you, Jim?"

Jim rubbed his temples for a moment and then threw his hands in the air. "Let's just agree to disagree, Malik. I'm done—"

"If we run out of firewood," Malik growled, with flames in his eyes, "I'm gonna snatch that flag off the wall and watch it burn! Put that thing to good use."

Jim waited in awkward silence for a few minutes. The wood crackled away in the fireplace. Malik's jaw eventually slackened.

"So," Jim finally asked, "what's the plan, Malik?"

Malik said nothing. His mouth twitched slightly. Jim continued. "Back when you first jumped in my car, I thought you might kill me with that gun. You scared me to death. I drove down that highway and listened to everything you said because I figured you could pull that trigger any minute. But shortly after we got here, I realized you weren't a killer. I don't believe you'll shoot me, Malik. It's the cold outside that's holding us both captive right now. But this freak storm is going to pass, and the temperatures are going to rise again. Then what?"

Malik frowned and kicked at a small coal that popped out near his foot. Jim kept talking. "I'm not going to stay here when it warms up. I'm going to go home and see my wife."

"You can leave whenever you want," Malik said. "I don't care."

"So what are you going to do? You can't stay here forever."

Malik shrugged. "The difference between you and me is you got something good to go home to. The police are waiting for me to turn back up because they think I'm one of the guys who rolled on my man, Habib. Those same cops want to lock my butt up for carjacking you too. So, there's that. But if they don't get me first, I still got three angry dudes who got a score to finish with me. So I ain't in much of a rush to get home, man. I think I'll just stay here . . ."

Jim weighed Malik's words for a moment. It confused him that this kid was talking like his life was over already. He looked at his watch. It was almost eight o'clock. He wasn't sure whether the sun would burn away the ice, and he wasn't certain there was enough gas in the car to get more than five miles down the gravel road and on the country highway; but his mind turned toward making a plan.

Malik took a look at the pile of logs left on the floor. There were five left.

17

THE LECTURE

8:37 a.m., Tuesday before Thanksgiving

DETECTIVE MARQUAN COLE COVERED HIS MOUTH for a yawn. He wandered slowly down the hallway with a few sips of lukewarm coffee left in a Styrofoam cup. A young lady in pajama pants and a goose-down jacket stood in the middle of the hall trying to pull on a pair of fluffy mittens.

"Excuse me," MarQuan asked. "Where is Lecture Hall Three?"

"Right around the corner there," the young woman said. She pointed to her right, a mitten still dangling off one of her hands.

"Thank you," he acknowledged with a slight nod. He followed her directions and found himself outside Lecture Hall Three. He slowly opened the door and quietly entered. A man's voice filled the large room. Close to one hundred students were scattered about. The auditorium was old, warm, and musty. MarQuan spotted a seat nearby and sat down.

Professor Keith Thompson was on a stage, seated behind a sizeable wooden desk, his notes scattered in front of him. He was winding down his lecture for his morning sociology course. "Violence is a curious thing," he said, lowering his head and peering over his glasses at the class. "We should rarely condone it or excuse it. But recent times have caused us to think about it more thoroughly, haven't they? Particularly when we think about violence within our communities. Many of us are befuddled by some of the recent incidents of police brutality toward people of color. We've all seen the news or the YouTube videos, haven't we? A lot of people are upset that the very ones hired to protect and serve are the same ones using their authority and power to abuse and to kill. Folks have rioted over these events, demonstrating violent behavior to let the police know that they're weary of the violence. Paradoxical behavior, some would say.

"Yet others would say, 'Yes. It's not right for the police to kill unarmed citizens, but what about when those same citizens are killing one another? Isn't it hypocritical to condemn one form of violence and yet say nothing about the other form?' What do you think?"

There was a silence in the room for a moment until a white kid with a ponytail raised his hand. Professor Thompson acknowledged him with a nod. "Patrick, you have a thought on this?"

The kid squirmed in his seat for a minute and cleared his throat. "Yeah, I guess it bothers me. I mean, I don't think it's right that there are police killing unarmed people. It also seems like the majority of people that they're killing are black people. I don't think that's right either. But I don't understand how people can riot and loot and make a big fuss over police brutality when, statistically speaking, the homicide rates are a lot higher in black communities than they are anywhere else. Police aren't the only ones killing black people." Patrick paused for a moment, choosing his words carefully. "If black lives matter—and they do—then it should matter whether it's the police taking those lives or another black person. I think you need to have it both ways. I mean—that's just my opinion, I guess."

The professor smiled. "Thank you, Patrick. Does anyone else want to chime in?" A slim black girl in the front of the room quickly raised her hand. "Yes, Carolyn?"

"I hear what Patrick is saying," she started. "I agree— somewhat. I don't agree with all the rioting and nonsense. Destroying your own neighborhood seems like a child having a tantrum. It's embarrassing.

"But on the other hand, we aren't just dealing with some isolated incidents here. I mean, there have been hundreds of years of this type of stuff. It was like, what, fifty or sixty years ago that black boys were lynched just for whistling at a white girl. Police sprayed some of our grandparents with fire hoses and loosed angry dogs on them because they were just trying to vote. I mean, that wasn't that long ago at all. Seems like we forget that this kinda stuff has been going on for a real long time. Blacks and other minorities are just tired of it.

"So, I'm not saying that the riots and all of that stuff are okay, but I understand that folks are angry. I'm angry too." Professor Thompson raised his eyebrows, urging her to continue. Carolyn rapped her pen on her desk for a moment and elaborated further. "I mean, I agree with what Patrick said about black-on-black crime. I think it's disingenuous to hate on the police for killing a black person but say next to nothing about a black person shooting another black person in the same neighborhood. That's hypocritical. But I'll say this: I think when people start shooting their own kind it indicates that community is hopeless.

"I mean, didn't Japanese soldiers kill themselves at the end of World War II when it was pretty much all over? You don't start killing your own, or killing yourself, until you've given up. I think a lot of these communities are looking around them and they see a jacked-up system—a jacked-up world—and they're just losing all hope."

"Thank you, Carolyn," the professor said with a nod. "Anyone else?" Quiet lingered in the lecture hall, aside from the old heat pipes groaning in the walls. "Class is almost over. So I'll wrap us up with this: As I said earlier, violence is a curious thing, and it requires great scrutiny. On one hand, it is the currency of the powerful, of the bully, of the agitator. We see this with some of our police. But we also see it with the gangbangers and thugs, right? Violence in the hands of either can be used to abuse, to agitate, to coerce, and to kill.

"But violence is also the cry of the dying and of the downtrodden. It's a last gasp, as Carolyn said, of a community that's losing—or lost—its hope. As Patrick said, there is a higher rate of murder in our urban black communities. Statistics bear that out. But let me make a few comments about that observation.

"One, there's a lot of buzz out there about 'black-on-black' crime. What we mean by that is 'blacks hurting or killing or robbing other blacks,' correct? But almost all crimes are committed against people who look the same. We still live in a predominantly segregated and homogeneous world. Most of us grew up in and still live in communities where people are ethnically the same. This classroom is fairly diverse, but I'm confident most of you don't live in a neighborhood that looks like this, do you?

"And so, most crimes are committed against people of the same ethnic origin. Most black crimes are against black people. Why? Because most black people live in an all-black neighborhood. But the same is true of white crime. We don't hear much about white-on-white crime or Korean-on-Korean crime, do we? But white people commit most of the robberies, drug deals, and murders that take place in white neighborhoods. Makes sense, doesn't it? And statistically, crime rates in black and white neighborhoods are relatively the same per capita. Just as many drugs are sold in the suburbs as are sold in the hood. But violent crime and murder are the categories that tend to stand out in our urban communities.

"Sociologists have done a lot to study these unique

statistics. They've uncovered some interesting things. There's one striking corollary with incidents of violence—I don't suppose you know what it is." He paused briefly and continued. "The murder rate and incidents of violence tend to spike almost universally in communities that have been devastated by poverty, unemployment, and—as Carolyn pointed out a moment ago—hopelessness.

"A professor at Harvard—Dr. Robert Sampson—calls this phenomenon 'compounded deprivation.' The majority of our urban communities are denied access to important lifelines that contribute to thriving communities: namely, jobs, strong schools, healthy food options, valuable property, and a prosperous business sector. In turn, these communities are overwhelmed with poverty, broken families, failing schools, illiteracy, and the mass incarceration of their men." Professor Thompson held up his arms to add emphasis. "So on one hand, these neighborhoods are under-resourced with basic necessities. On the other hand, they're saturated with adversities. How can such a community ever survive, let alone thrive?" His question hung in the air for a moment as Professor Thompson stroked his thick beard thoughtfully.

"Perhaps I can illustrate," he continued. "You probably can't picture it, but I used to be quite the basketball player. I still hold the all-time rebound record for my old high school. But back in the day there was a kid named James Sanderson. He was six-and-a-half feet tall. James was the smoothest high school player I've ever seen. No one could stop him. Literally no one. He used to come into our gym with his team and humiliate us. We'd double-team him and he'd still score over thirty points a game—in our own house, no less. He'd run his mouth, beat his chest, and rile up our fans with his trash talk. But there was no way to stop James. We could only try to slow him down. In the four times I faced him, I fouled out every game before the fourth quarter started. I was completely helpless and hopeless to stop him, and I absolutely dreaded playing him.

"But we had a kid on our team named Isaiah Jenkins. Isaiah couldn't hoop to save his life, but he wasn't one to trifle with. It was senior year, and James was having one of his nights—just killin' us. He received a technical for cussing out our bench. Toward the end of the game, he was on a breakaway for one of his signature dunks. But then ol' Isaiah took him out with one of the nastiest and most flagrant fouls I've ever witnessed. James landed on his back and stayed there for a while. Isaiah had knocked him out cold. Someone asked Isaiah about it later. He said, 'I decided to stop him the only way I knew how.'" A handful of nervous chuckles echoed in the lecture hall.

"Now," the professor asked, leaning over his desk. "Is what Isaiah did right?"

A few students shook their heads, but no one spoke.

"Of course it wasn't right," Professor Thompson said, answering his own question. "But in a weird kind of way, does it make sense? Isaiah responded the only way he knew how against a superior opponent. So, what about the James Sandersons in some of our communities? Take poverty, for instance. That's a real tough opponent, isn't it? But some-times poverty teams up with police profiling and brutality. That makes things even tougher. What about if you add joblessness and mass incarceration, or failing schools where fewer than 30 percent of kids even graduate? What if the chief breadwinners in your community are in jail or have gotten out of jail and no one will hire them?

"It's tough enough to face one James Sanderson—an opponent who beats you every time and humiliates you while doing it. What about if you're playing a whole team of Sandersons? How long is it before you respond like Isaiah Jenkins and lash out?"

The clock in the back of the room caught the professor's eye. He winced. Time was almost up.

"Violent crime," he said, beginning to wrap up quickly, "is impossible to condone. But when it surfaces in certain communities more than others, it's important to try and diagnose why. Some simply label things quickly and try to connect violence to race rather than to circumstances or context. The reality is that any community—regardless of race—that is facing the James Sandersons of poverty, jobless-ness, and brokenness tends to use violence in equal measure. In most cases, when violence emerges in a community, it has become the currency of negotiation for people who feel like they have no other option." He paused for a moment, then slapped his desk with a smile. "I wish we had more time to discuss this! But the class is over—and I need to grab some coffee! Don't forget to read chapter two in *The New*

Jim Crow. And remember, your essays are due next Monday. Enjoy some turkey and stay safe! Class dismissed."

The students stood, gathered their things, zipped up their coats, and headed for the exit. Detective Cole waited for the last student to leave before descending the stairs toward the stage. He clapped his hands slowly. The professor looked up from stuffing his papers in his satchel. "Pro-fess-or Keith Thompson!" Detective Cole said with a warm laugh. "That was a riveting lecture, brother."

Keith squinted over his glasses, until a wide smile curled across his face. "Is that you, MarQuan? What in the world brings you here?"

MarQuan jogged up the steps of the stage and walked toward his old friend. Keith pushed himself away from his desk. MarQuan tried not to stare at the wheelchair. He leaned down and gave his old friend a hug. "How are you, man?" He leaned back up and folded his arms across his chest. "I haven't seen you in almost ten years."

"I've been better," Keith replied, with a pained expression. "I suppose you heard about my little accident."

MarQuan grimaced slightly. "Yeah. I heard. I'm sorry I haven't come by till now."

Keith waved his hand. "Everyone is busy—especially a world-famous detective like you." They both laughed as Keith continued. "I'm glad to see you. But I'm nervous—I always knew that what I did back in sixth grade would come back to haunt me someday . . ." He let out an awkward laugh.

MarQuan responded with a weak smile. "You said you

needed a cup of coffee. I do too. Is there somewhere we could go?"

"There's a pot in my office right now. Want to push me there?"

. . .

Moments later, Keith poured a cup for MarQuan, wheeled around slowly, and handed it to him. "So, why are you here?" He blew some steam off the top of his cup before setting it down on his desk.

MarQuan attempted a sip and flinched before setting his cup down on the seat next to him. He took a moment to admire all of the books on the professor's shelves. On the wall was a purple heart in a frame, next to the doctorate degree Keith had received from Brown. "You've read all these books?" MarQuan asked.

"A book doesn't make it on my shelf unless I've read it."

"Or wrote it, I see." MarQuan pointed at a few volumes.

"Come on, man. Why are you here?"

MarQuan let out a slight sigh. "It's your nephew Malik."

Keith's eyes widened, and he pulled his glasses from his face. "Did he get arrested? Tell me that boy didn't do something stupid, MarQuan."

"He's missing, Keith."

"Missing?" Keith replied. "What does that mean?"

MarQuan shook his head. "We don't really know. Yesterday evening your mom sent him out for some groceries. There was some kind of incident between him and three other boys. One of them jumped the cashier and beat him up pretty badly. An eyewitness in the parking lot saw a kid jump in a black Lexus sedan and drive off. The other three boys disappeared into the community."

Keith was stunned. He absentmindedly pulled his hand through his thick black beard but said nothing.

"But things get stranger, Keith. A white attorney from Stone Brook has disappeared too."

"I don't get it."

"He and some folks from his church have been delivering groceries to your mom for the last couple of months. He came by yesterday and dropped off some things for Thanksgiving. He never made it home."

Keith shook his head. "Well, some of the roads had ice on them last night . . ."

"I checked with all the police reports from accidents on the highways and roads from Edgewood to Stone Brook. There was a fair share of accidents last night, but none involving a black Lexus sedan."

"You don't think Malik carjacked him or something?" Keith growled. "Malik has done some stupid things, but he wouldn't do anything like that—no sir!"

"When's the last time you've seen your nephew, Keith?" MarQuan attempted another sip of coffee but gave up again.

Keith stared off for a moment before responding. "Probably about eight months ago. I don't know—I used to swing by and check up on him once or twice a month before the accident. But since then I've done a poor job staying in touch."

MarQuan interlaced his fingers and twirled his thumbs. He glanced out the window and watched as the bundled students bowed their heads in the cold and crossed the snowy campus lawn. From up in the office, they looked like sheep.

"What have you uncovered so far?" Keith asked.

MarQuan frowned. "Not a whole lot. The boys back at the department have been reviewing the camera footage from the convenience store, but it's very grainy. It's tough to tell if the four guys in the store were friends or not. Most of what we've got is from the forensic team at the crime scene. One of the guys in the store assaulted the cashier with a beer bottle and beat him pretty badly. Last I heard he's still unconscious. If he wakes up, I'm sure he can help us understand a little more of what happened. Shortly after the assault, one of the kids tossed a gallon of milk on the floor and took off running. Then the other three ran out as well. There's a lot of different ways to interpret what happened in there."

"So," Keith asked, taking another cautious sip of his coffee. "Are you trying to find a criminal or a missing person?"

"Could be both," MarQuan replied.

Keith's voice softened. "Everybody sticks up for his or her family. But I've known Malik since the day he was born. His mama, my sister Sobrina, is a lost cause. His dad is a crackhead, and no one's seen him in about six years. But Malik's always been different. He used to spend entire summers with me here at the college, attending summer workshops, studying and growing. He's one of the top kids in his class. He's learned from the mistakes he made along the way. He's seen his parents ruin their lives and always tried to be better. He's a great example for his younger siblings, and I'm proud of him. Sure, he's capable of stupid, but he's not a robber and a carjacker." Keith looked up from his desk and stared his old friend in the eyes. "I can tell you that for certain."

"I hope you're right," MarQuan said, as he retrieved his cup of coffee and stood to his feet. "You mind if I keep this for the road? I don't have a Harpers College mug."

"Sure," Keith replied. "Look, I appreciate you driving out here to see me and to keep me in the loop. Mama will probably call me in another day or two. She's always kept bad news to herself for as long she can."

MarQuan grabbed the office door to leave. "Good seeing you, Keith," he said.

"MarQuan," Keith said sternly.

MarQuan spun back around. "Yeah. What is it?"

"Find my nephew first," Keith said. His voice trembled just slightly. "If he's messed up in this at all—even if he isn't—I need for *you* to find him first and bring him in."

A pained and knowing expression flashed across the detective's face. He nodded at the professor and closed the door.

18

THE MEAL

10:37 a.m., Tuesday before Thanksgiving

SUNLIGHT FILLED THE CABIN. The snow was no longer falling outside. The trees glistened with ice. Malik stood wide-eyed, admiring the marvelous scene just outside the window.

Jim leaned back in his chair and checked his watch: 10:37. His stomach growled violently.

Malik turned and furrowed his brow. "Dang. Sounded like a grizzly bear."

Jim clutched his belly and shook his head. "I'm so hungry."

Malik sighed. "I know, right? Maybe there's something this redneck left in these cupboards over here?"

Jim shook his head. "I doubt it."

Malik walked over to the old, dilapidated cupboards and cautiously opened them. His eyes lit up. "Man, homie has some Viennas!"

Jim shot him a quizzical glance. "What's a Vie-yeena?"

"Come on, man!" Malik pulled the can from the cupboard and held it out. "You've never had Viennas before?"

Jim stood up and walked over to Malik. He took the can from his hand and studied it before shaking his head. "'Vienna sausages.' No. I've never had these. What do you call them, again?"

"Vie-yeenas."

"Vie-yeenas?" Jim imitated cautiously.

Malik nodded.

"Okay," Jim said with a shrug. "Do they taste good? Actually, I don't really care. I could eat almost anything right now."

Malik nodded, peeled back the tab on the can, and extracted a sausage. Jim eyed the small piece of meat in Malik's hand. A curious clear liquid was drizzling off it back into the can. Malik popped it into his mouth and chewed. He nodded his head up and down. "Yes sir!" he chirped with a rapturous look on his face.

"That good, huh?" Jim said with squinted eyes. "What's the weird jelly stuff those things are swimming in?"

Malik shrugged. "Dunno. It's good though. You better snag you one or I'll crush this whole can." He popped another sausage in his mouth.

Jim looked at Malik, at the can, back at Malik, and then slowly pulled a sausage from the can. He jiggled it over the can, trying to shake as much liquid off it as possible. Malik watched excitedly as Jim placed the sausage in his mouth and slowly chewed. "Good, isn't it?" Malik asked hopefully.

"It's food I guess," Jim said glumly. "A little bit slimy and salty for me."

Malik frowned and shook his head. "Maybe it would taste better if you could dip it in some hummus? That's cool if you don't like 'em. Means there's more for me then."

Jim sighed and opened the cupboard. He was disappointed to see three more cans of the canned meat and nothing else. Reluctantly he grabbed one and opened it.

"There you go!" Malik said. "Get you some."

"Desperate times call for desperate measures," Jim mumbled. He took his can and walked back toward the fire.

"Hey!" Malik hollered after him. "Don't throw those Viennas in the fire, man! I know you're tired, but don't do nothin' crazy."

Jim leaned down and snatched a stick off the floor near the log pile. Squeamishly he removed another sausage and pierced it on the end of the thin branch. Malik watched curiously as Jim held the stick over the coal bed and slowly rotated it. The tiny sausage quickly browned and wilted over the heat. After a minute Jim pulled it from the coals and blew on it before popping it into his mouth. He smiled. "Much better," he said. He pulled another sausage from the can and repeated the process.

Malik walked briskly over to the fireplace and stood next to Jim. "Yo. That ain't a bad idea. I'm gonna heat up my sausage over here too."

Jim glanced up with a curious grin on his face. Malik looked at him strangely for a moment before shaking his head and bursting into laughter.

"You're hilarious, dude. You know what I mean."

The two of them sat side by side, leaning over the coals, heating their breakfast. The aromatic smell of roasted meat filled the cabin as each sausage filled their stomachs.

■　■　■

"I can't believe Thanksgiving is in two days," Jim said wistfully. He leaned back from the fire and wiped the corner of his mouth with his thumb.

"Yeah, me neither," Malik replied. He popped another sausage into his mouth.

"You guys have some family traditions?" Jim asked.

Malik chewed for a moment and gave a slight shrug. "I guess. As long as I can remember, we've always had Thanksgiving at my grandma's. She usually does most of the cookin'. My mom, her sister LeKeisha, my Uncle Keith, and his son, Camron, usually drop by. They typically bring some kinda fixin' with them."

"What's your favorite part of the meal?"

"Outside of the turkey, it's hard not to like my grandma's greens. And my Uncle Keith makes some pretty good chitlins."

"Chitlins, huh?" Jim cocked his head to the side. "For Thanksgiving? I've never heard of that one before."

"Throw some hot sauce on them and you're good to go,"

Malik said with a slight nod. "Hot sauce on your greens too—delicious!"

"Never heard of hot sauce at Thanksgiving, either."

"Not everybody eats hummus," Malik mumbled.

"All right. Enough with the hummus jokes," Jim said. "That's not the only thing white folks eat."

"Yeah? But did y'all have some at Thanksgiving last year?"

Jim cleared his throat. "I don't remember . . . maybe as an appetizer or something . . . I've never had chitlins before. Are they really good?"

Malik nodded. "Yeah man. They're good if they're done right. My Uncle Keith used to make them on some special occasions. He said he had some kinda secret ingredient. But after the accident two years ago, he stopped makin' them, so—"

"Accident?"

■ ■ ■

Malik stared out the window of Aunt LeKeisha's car. The rain thudded loudly on the roof.

"Come on, people!" his aunt shouted. She laid on the horn. "How come everybody forgets how to drive when it storms?" Cars crawled slowly down the road. Malik leaned forward in his seat. Through the torrential sheets of water he could see the hospital lights up ahead. His aunt cursed and laid on the horn again.

"Be calm, LeKeisha," Malik's grandma said. "You're gonna cause another accident." She placed her hand softly on her daughter's knee.

Malik sucked in his lips and winced. His head throbbed. It had been throbbing ever since his mom answered their phone, shrieked, and collapsed onto the couch with her face in her hands. No matter how many times he asked what was wrong, she continued to sit there, shaking her head with her legs trembling. She stayed that way until his aunt pulled up to the house. "Come on, baby," she had said to him, frowning at his mom as she took his hand. "Uncle Keith is in the hospital. Leave your mama here. We gotta go."

Finally they reached the hospital. With quick and deliberate steps, they rushed down the bright white hallways until they found Uncle Keith's room. LeKeisha barged in, nearly knocking a nurse to the ground. Malik's grandmother whispered a prayer and entered slowly. But Malik felt his feet freeze. He wanted to go no further. Fear paralyzed him.

"Oh my God!" his aunt bellowed. "Keith! Keith!"

A voice from behind Malik spoke assuredly. "It's okay, son." He turned to see the weary face of a doctor. He tried to muster a half-smile. The doctor placed his hand on Malik's elbow and drew him into the room.

Malik lost his breath as he spotted his uncle hooked up to a variety of machines. He was unconscious, and his face was shrouded in bloodied bandages. Malik's grandmother was already at Keith's bedside, holding his hand as tears streamed down her face. Aunt LeKeisha continued to cry out his name. Malik just stood there in the middle of the room, staring at his uncle's motionless frame.

"Hello," the doctor said. "I'm Dr. Carlson." His voice captured everyone's attention. "Mr. Thompson was hit by a drunk driver leaving campus this evening."

"Drunk driver?" LeKeisha's face twisted with contempt. "A drunk driver did this to him?" The doctor nodded.

"Is he going to live?" Malik's grandmother asked cautiously.

The doctor nodded. "We think so. But his injuries are severe. He has a concussion, three cracked ribs, and . . . it's unknown if he'll have use of his legs again."

Malik's eyes widened, and he felt his stomach twist. "You mean," his grandmother asked, "he ain't gonna walk again?"

Dr. Carlson grimaced. "It's doubtful. The damage to his spine is substantial."

"What about the other driver?" LeKeisha retorted. "I hope he's laid up in a bed here too. Or maybe he's dead?"

"LeKeisha!" her mother shouted.

"No, Mama. I want to know if this drunk piece of trash is okay too!"

"He's with the police," the doctor said. "His injuries were superficial."

"Oh my God!" LeKeisha roared. "I hope they lock his sorry—"

"Look," Dr. Carlson interrupted. "Mr. Thompson is going to need all of you. His life is going to be very different now, and the support of his family is absolutely crucial. Is he married? Does he have any kids?"

Malik's aunt threw herself down in a chair and just stared out the window as the rain continued to fall in thick sheets.

His grandmother shook her head. "No. He's divorced, and his ex-wife lives in Tennessee somewhere. His son isn't around now either. We're all he has right now."

"Well," Dr. Carlson replied plainly, "he's going to need all of you to be strong."

■ ■ ■

Jim frowned. "I'm sorry to hear about your Uncle Keith. What's he up to now?"

Malik shrugged. "He's a strong man. He got out of the hospital, did a lot of rehab, and he's back wheeling himself around in the classroom at the college where he works."

"Does he still come to see you?"

"He can't drive. Grandma doesn't have a car, and no one else from my family is really willin' to make the trip out there to get him. So no, not really."

"Did anything ever happen to the guy who hit him?" Jim asked.

"Not really," Malik replied. "He was some college kid driving back to his dorm from a frat party. My uncle was working late and was on his way home. The kid hit my uncle going thirty-five miles over the speed limit. His dad is a big-shot lawyer or something. I think they worked it out for him to do community service or something. But that's about it. He snatched my uncle's legs from him—and pretty much snatched my uncle from my family too."

"Did you mention a cousin?" Jim queried.

Malik nodded. "Yeah. Camron."

Jim waited a moment, then prodded further. "What's up with him?"

"He's still got one more year on his sentence. He's Uncle Keith's only son—been locked up for two years for possession. He was busted a second time for weed."

"Dealing drugs, huh?"

"Nah," Malik continued. "Camron's no dealer. He smokes the stuff on occasion. One day he got pulled over for some bull, and they found weed on him. Because he was within a thousand feet of a school or whatever, they locked him away for three years. He's never dealt drugs in his life— but that ain't what the prosecution said." Malik shook his head. "It's funny now that I think about it. Some college boy got drunk and leaves my uncle in a wheelchair, and the courts tell him he needs to pick up trash for a few weeks to make up for his mistakes. Camron hasn't hurt a fly but just has some weed in his pocket on the wrong day, and they lock him up for three years. I guess that's how the system works though, right?"

"When you put it like that," Jim said thoughtfully, "it's not right. A drunken kid speeding in a car is far more dangerous than someone with weed in his pocket. I'm not saying weed in any circumstance is okay, but there's no way your cousin deserves a harsher consequence than the kid who hit your uncle. The punishment should suit the crime."

"I usually just get mad about it all, man," Malik said, pursing his lips. "You got police choking a dude to death for selling cigarettes. You got police shootin' unarmed kids and leaving their bodies in the streets. But no one pays for it—no one is accountable except the ones lyin' dead on the concrete. Then you got white boys drivin' around drunk in their daddy's Benz and white folks sniffin' coke up in the burbs, and nobody cares about that for real. But a young black kid like Camron with weed in his pocket? Shoot! He's the menace to society. We got to get his dangerous butt off of the streets and lock him up! If life is a game, then the game is rigged, man! Uncle Keith said it's like trying to play basketball and foulin' out of the game with the first foul. But then some of these white folks out here get seven or eight fouls!" Malik dropped his head. "My dad fouled out. My cousin Ricky fouled out. No sayin' what Camron will do once he gets out, but unless there's some kind of miracle, he's probably fouled out already. Me too! You think anyone is gonna believe I'm innocent . . . that circumstances last night forced me to do what I did?" Malik looked desperately at Jim to say something, but he said nothing. "No!" Malik cried. "No one would believe a word I said, because I'm already who they think I am." Malik held his hand up and started lifting his fingers one at a time. "I'm black. Male. Hood. Dangerous." He looked at Jim. "Maybe now you're startin' to understand why I don't have a lot of hope for my situation."

Jim was quiet for a moment. "What about your uncle," he finally asked. "Has he lost hope?"

"Uncle Keith used to hope. He said a broken system

could be fixed if everyone could just admit that it was
broken and then work together to make it right. He always
had this belief deep inside of him that anything that is
broken can be restored. But when he lost his legs, and when
the system that he hoped could be fixed took his son, it
kinda snatched his hope as well. Uncle Keith isn't the type
to fold, but he doesn't have much left to play with, either."

Jim sniffed and tightened his lips. He stared absently
into the dying coals of the fire. From outside the cabin, they
noticed a crunching noise in the distance, coming closer.

Malik sprang from his seat and raced to the window.
He pulled back the tattered curtain to peer outside. With a
desperate movement he pulled his gun from out of the back
of his pants.

"What's wrong?" Jim asked as he slowly rose from his chair.

Malik stood transfixed, staring out the window. He spoke
in a frightened whisper. "Someone is coming."

19

THE INTRUDER

11:12 a.m., Tuesday before Thanksgiving

JIM STOOD NEXT TO MALIK at the window and watched as a rusted green pickup truck approached the cabin. Thick gray exhaust puffed from the pipe in the back, rolling atop the glistening ice in an ominous cloud.

Malik stood like a statue—aside from the gun that shook in his hand. This was the first sign of life either of them had seen in over twelve hours, but Jim did not like the look of this truck. He, too, felt his stomach tightening.

"Ah, man." Malik looked at the two stickers on the truck's sagging rear bumper. "Trump and the Confederate flag . . . This ain't good at all."

"Look," Jim said loudly. "We just need to stay calm. You need to put that gun up, Malik. Whoever this is will not respond well if they see you carrying a gun."

The truck rumbled closer and parked about fifty yards away from the cabin. The windshield of the vehicle was cracked, and through it they could see the silhouette of the driver. An eternity seemed to pass as they waited for something to happen. The man remained in his truck while it sputtered loudly, continuing to unleash gray smog that refused to dissipate in the frigid morning air.

"What's he waitin' on?" Malik whispered. "Why's he just sittin' there? How'd he know we were here?"

"He probably saw the smoke from the fire," Jim replied. "Maybe I should go out there and talk to him."

"No. You crazy?" Malik said. "We need to stay right here."

Finally the driver-side door opened. An older man in camouflage stepped slowly out of the truck and into the icy snow. A long, silvery beard hung down on his chest. With his gloved hands he gave his bright orange stocking cap a tug. He reached into his truck and pulled out a hunting rifle and placed it on his shoulder. A large, spotted dog bounded out of the vehicle, panting excitedly.

Malik's eyes widened even more, and he trembled noticeably as the man and his dog approached the cabin. Jim looked at Malik and then out of the window again. "Listen, Malik," he said calmly, "you need to go and hide. Go hide in the bathroom or something." Uncertainty darted in Jim's eyes. "I'll think of something."

Malik replied tersely. "You'll probably just hand me over to this dude or let his dog get me. I ain't about to let that happen."

"Listen!" Jim barked. "Do you trust me or that man out there more? I realize this feels like a lose-lose, but you need to trust me. We're both trespassing right now, and this man may not take too kindly to that."

Malik looked at Jim with desperation in his eyes. He didn't know whom he could trust at the moment, but somehow the last sixteen hours with Jim mattered. He took a step back from the window and hurried to the bathroom. He looked at Jim one more time before pulling the door shut, just as a loud knock shook the door of the cabin.

Jim swallowed. His legs felt heavy as he plodded toward the front door. He didn't know why he was afraid—he hadn't done anything wrong, other than try to stay alive. Surely this visitor would understand that a man would need shelter on a cold night like the last one. But at the same time, Jim didn't like the look of this man. He wasn't sure that he would help at all. He grabbed the handle and slowly pulled open the door. "Morning," Jim said as confidently as he could.

Malik sat on the toilet lid, the 9mm trained in front of him. He leaned forward, trying to hear the conversation.

The man at the door had a craggy and weather-beaten face. His eyes were dark and partially concealed behind large, unruly eyebrows. His dog sat on its haunches, its head cocked sideways. "You a friend of Bert's?" the old man asked, shrugging slightly to adjust the rifle on his shoulder.

Jim shook his head. "No. I don't know Bert."

"Well," the old man replied. "This is his cabin. Why you in Bert's cabin?"

"I got lost last night and found this hunting camp," Jim said. "I didn't want to die of cold, so I decided to crash here and stay warm."

The old man leaned forward, trying to peer inside. "I saw you drive in last night. You drive a fancy-boy car, son. What are you and your fancy-boy car doing way out here, anyways?"

Jim thought quickly. "I'm an insurance adjustor. I have a client out here somewhere with roof damage. The weather turned nasty last night, and I got turned around. The GPS isn't all that useful out here. When I saw the sign for the hunting camp, I thanked the Lord—I was doubting whether or not I'd make it home. I'm hoping to get out of here today if I can. Do I need to leave Bert a check or something for the firewood I used?"

"Mind if I come in?" The man stuck one of his heavy boots inside with a thud. Jim cleared out of his way as the old man and his dog stepped into the cabin.

"I didn't catch your name," Jim said with a half-smile.

"I didn't catch yours either."

"Jim Dawson." Jim extended his hand. Another quick lie. The dog growled slightly.

"Easy, Lilac." The man placed his hand on the dog's head. "My name is Tucker," he said to Jim. "But everyone around here calls me Bug. I'm the manager of this property and live here year-round."

"Okay, Bug," Jim replied slowly. "Nice to meet you."

"You got someone else here with you, Jim?" Bug asked with a raised eyebrow.

"No. Just me."

"Hmmm." Bug clomped over to the fireplace. "Looks like you're on your last two pieces of firewood." He paused for a moment, resting his hands on both of the chairs. "You know it got down to minus three degrees last night? Minus three degrees! Never been that cold down here before—not since I've been alive anyways."

Jim nodded and watched as the old man moved slowly around the cabin. Lilac clung close to his heels and nosed through the sausage cans on the floor. A coal popped in the fireplace and gave the dog a start. "Is the weather supposed to warm up today?" Jim asked.

Bug offered up a grin, revealing some missing teeth. "Yeah. If you call thirty-eight degrees warming up."

"Well, that's good," Jim responded. "Maybe I can get out of here this afternoon, then."

"Maybe," the old man said. "There's definitely gonna be some ice in a few places."

Lilac stopped. Her ears perked slightly, and she turned her attention toward the bathroom. Jim noticed and looked over at Bug. He was staring back at Jim with a strange expression.

"Do you have any more firewood in the back of your truck that I could use?" Jim asked. "As I said, I'd like to be out of here as soon as the temperatures rise a little bit, but I could use some more wood in the meanwhile."

Bug looked at Jim, over at the bathroom, and then back at Jim. He called his dog and moved back toward the front door again. "Jim," he said gruffly, spinning around to face him from in front of the doorway. "I don't know who you are or why you're here. But I can spot a liar when I see one, and you ain't no insurance adjustor. My guess? You're one of them meth dealers, or something like that. We've had a few of them up here over the years, cookin' and sellin' that mess. All I know is you ain't no adjustor and you bein' all the way out here in your fancy car doesn't make any sense to me." He cast a quick glance toward the bathroom. "And you ain't here alone, neither."

With that, he opened the door and slammed it behind him. He trudged rapidly back to his truck, still puttering out front.

Malik burst out of the bathroom with his gun still drawn. "Is he gone? Finally, man!" He pulled back the curtain again and peeked out the window. "That dude was like something out of a horror movie, for real! Thanks for covering for me—I appreciate it."

"I don't like to lie," Jim muttered. "But I didn't feel right about him for one minute."

From behind the tattered curtain they both watched Bug pause outside of his truck. He pulled a glove off of his hand with his teeth and retrieved his cell phone from his pocket.

"Who do you think he's calling?" Malik asked.

Jim spoke quietly. "Probably the police."

20

THE DECISION

12:19 p.m., Tuesday before Thanksgiving

THE OLD MAN HAD MADE HIS CALL and returned to his truck. He rumbled back down the snow-laden road before pulling off into a driveway, where he still sat, monitoring the cabin for the last thirty minutes. Malik paced nervously back and forth. Meanwhile, Jim's attention remained fixed outside the window. Now and then he glanced at his watch.

"Man!" Malik suddenly erupted. "I ain't gonna just sit here and wait for somethin' to happen. If that old dude called the police, then I need to get up and out of here. Now!"

Jim took a look at the gun in Malik's hand and the panic in his eyes. "The best thing to do right now, Malik, is stop and think. If you keep running, your situation is only going to get worse. You already ran once. Besides, these roads are still a mess, and there's nowhere for you to go. You wouldn't make it more than a few miles down the road before you crashed or ran out of gas. You need to think this through."

"So you think I should just stick around and wait for some country crackerjack police officers to show up and arrest me?" Malik growled with a furrowed brow. "'Cause that ain't happenin'!"

"Then what's the plan, Malik?" Jim retorted. "I've been asking you that all night. Are you going to shoot your way out, go live in the woods somewhere? I mean, what is it? What did you think was going to happen? Did you think that this whole mess would just blow over—that people would just forget or something? You can't win this one."

"Win?" Malik shouted. "Win? Man, I ain't tryin' to win. I'm just tryin' to stay alive. I've already told you that I've lost. Don't you think I've thought about my situation a few times over the last few hours? Assault. Robbery. Carjacking. Kidnapping. And now you add breaking and entering, or trespassing, or whatever. Any one of those charges will put me away for a while, right? There ain't no way to come out of this a winner!"

Jim shook his head and took a step forward. "The best thing you could do is just give me that gun and then let things unfold. If what you said is true about what happened back in that gas station, then you'll have your chance to prove it."

"Because they'll listen to my side of the story, right? Who else is gonna testify for me? Mike and his boys? You? Are you gonna be my lawyer, Jim? Shoot! The only person that could speak up for me is probably dead. And some folks think I'm the one who killed him. Look—I might as well just go ahead and walk down to the jail and lock myself up for the next twenty years, because that's what they're gonna do anyways!"

Jim could tell that he wasn't getting through. He took another look out of the window. Bug was still parked in the distance. The fire had died, and the cabin was rapidly growing colder.

Malik closed his eyes and tried to breath slowly. He could feel his heartbeats thudding against the walls of his chest, could hear them ricocheting around in his head.

Suddenly Jim leaned forward. Another vehicle was coming their way, a lone white SUV. It crawled down the long road before pausing in front of Bug's truck. On top of the truck was a rack of lights. It was the county sheriff.

Jim hoped Malik wouldn't notice, but the young man was now standing beside him, peering out of the window. Bug had stepped out of his truck and approached the sheriff's vehicle. He pointed toward the cabin.

Jim turned to say something, but Malik had already bolted toward the back door. Jim froze for a moment, wondering where Malik was going to go. But then he recalled that he had left his keys in the dash holder. He sprang toward the back as well.

Malik was already inside the Lexus and fumbling for the keys. "Come on, Malik!" Jim shouted. "Don't be stupid! Where are you going to go? What are you going to do?"

Malik ignored him and slammed the driver-side door

shut. For reasons he couldn't explain, Jim raced around the front of the car and opened the passenger door. Malik had already found the key and placed it in the ignition.

"Listen!" Jim yelled. "This will only make things ten times worse than they are."

"Things can't get no worse!" Malik retorted as he fired up the engine.

Jim looked off into the distance for a moment and then back at the young man who was struggling to get the car into drive. "Do you even know what you're doing?" The car had spent the night under an umbrella of pine trees; the ground had nothing more than a thin layer of powdery snow on it. Malik placed his gun in his lap and gripped the steering wheel with both hands, when it dawned on him that the entire front windshield was covered in ice.

Malik cursed and fumbled to find the driver-side window control. With a slight groan the window dropped, and he stuck his head outside. He took his foot off of the brake, and the car rolled forward.

Jim jogged alongside the car for a moment, yelling at Malik to stop, but Malik ignored him, navigating the car around the edge of the cabin and onto the snow-covered driveway. He could barely breathe. The icy air lashed against his face and burned his lungs. The frozen steering wheel felt foreign in his hands; the engine drew him onward with an unrestrained power.

Jim continued to run alongside the car as it picked up speed. Half out of anger and half out of desperation, he leaped into the passenger seat and slammed the door. "Pull over and put the car in park!" he said forcefully. "This is going to end with you totaling this car and winding up in a hospital."

They slowly rounded the corner and spotted the police vehicle and Bug in the distance. Malik pressed his foot down on the gas pedal; he had made his decision. Jim recognized that it was time for him to make his. He could jump out or stay put.

He reached for the door handle to attempt a hasty exit, but Malik depressed the gas pedal even more, throwing Jim into his seat as the car roared into action and raced forward. Jim frantically grabbed his seat belt and clicked it into place.

The sheriff and Bug stared at the Lexus as it kicked up a wake of white powder. Malik's squinting face still hung out of the driver side window. The car continued its rapid approach, and the sheriff put his hand on his holster. Bug sprang from the road and hid beside his truck. Malik grimaced.

"Be careful! Be careful!" Jim shouted. He placed his hands on the dash to brace himself.

The sheriff nearly toppled over as the Lexus raced past, missing him by inches. He reached for his gun for a moment but instead grabbed his radio and held it up to his mouth. "We have a black Lexus exiting Morgan's. License plate: One. Charlie. Alpha. Two. Four. Alpha. Delta. Driver is black. Male. Requesting immediate backup." He yanked open the door to his vehicle and jumped inside.

Jim spun around in his seat and watched as the SUV made a rapid three-point turn and began pursuit, its lights flashing and siren blaring. "Look," he asked desperately. "Just let me out!"

"Forget it!" Malik replied. "You shouldn't have jumped inside."

The road was blanketed in a thick layer of powder and a thin layer of ice, but the gravel provided great traction. Malik took a sharp left turn that would point them back toward the county highway. "This is ridiculous!" Jim said, shaking his head in disbelief. "Where in the world are you going to go? Do you really think this is going to work?"

Malik said nothing. He could hear Jim's voice, but his words were garbled. The frigid air continued to pummel his face and drown his ears. Outside, the world was white as far as he could see. Terror drove him onward. He had never felt so hopelessly alive.

Jim, on the other hand, sat there wide-eyed with his teeth clenched. He clung desperately to the roof handle with both hands.

21

THE CALL

12:53 p.m., Tuesday before Thanksgiving

THE SHRILL RING OF THE PHONE on the wall startled
Wilma. She released her grip on her cup of coffee. Exhaling
a slight sigh, she rose from her kitchen chair to catch the
phone before it rang a third time. "Hello?" she asked wearily.

"Hey, Ma," a voice on the other side said softly.

"Keith? Is that you?" A slight smile formed on Wilma's
lips. "How are you, baby?"

"I'm good, Ma." Keith sat behind his desk in his office.
His face rested in his hand. "MarQuan Cole came by this
morning. He told me about Malik."

Wilma winced but said nothing.

"Were you gonna call me, Ma?"

"I was, son," Wilma replied. "But you have enough on
your mind right now—enough going on. I was gonna give it

a day or two. Figured he'd turn up and we wouldn't need to bother you with it."

Keith closed his eyes and shook his head slightly. "Ma— you know that you and the family are never a bother. How are you and the kids holding up?"

"The babies don't know just yet," Wilma said. "They're playing next door this morning. I'm holding up—just here praying for Malik. Only Jesus knows where that boy is right now."

Keith turned slightly and took a look out of his office window. Large, fluffy clouds hung in the sharp blue sky. "MarQuan said Malik might be tangled up in some real mess. I can't see that boy doing anything like that—hurting anybody, stealing a car."

Wilma shook her head. "Me neither, son."

"So then, what's going on? Where is that boy, and what is he doing?"

Wilma shrugged. "I don't know, baby. I shouldn't have sent him out so late for those groceries. Lord knows it was getting dark and cold out there. Malik wouldn't hurt nobody. He must have gotten spooked or threatened by someone or something. That's the only reason he wouldn't come home."

"But what about that mess at the gas station?"

"Malik loves that place, Keith," Wilma replied. "You know that. He's known Habib since he was almost five. He wouldn't lay a finger on that man—or his store. You know this neighborhood. Anything could have happened. The best time of the day for me is when those four babies come home from school and they're safe and sound in my apartment. Every day there's another fight up at their schools, and every week it seems like there's another shooting. It's much worse than when you were a boy."

"You think he's mixed up with that white man who came to see you yesterday evening? Have they ever met before?"

"No," Wilma said plainly. "That was Jim's first time coming to our place. Him and Malik have never met before."

"Do you know what this Jim does for a living, Ma?" Keith queried. "He's a big-shot lawyer from Stone Brook. I truly hope that Malik has not done something foolish to or with a man like him."

"I know our Malik didn't do anything wrong, Keith. Besides, Jim seemed like a nice man. I don't think he did anything wrong either."

"So, Jim is from Mars? He's part of that group that's been bringing you the charity?"

"Don't say it like that," Wilma chided him. "Ain't no one from *my* church bringing us no groceries, son."

"They might if you would tell them you needed some."

"Just about every other person in our church needs some groceries or a power bill or something."

"Not your pastor," Keith retorted. "Pastor Jackson doesn't need anything. He and his Escalade seem to be doing just fine! I wonder if he's ever had trouble with his power bill or his groceries."

Keith's mother sniffed but said nothing. Keith continued.

"Besides, I've been trying to send you some money too. Is that not enough?"

Wilma nodded. "Every bit helps, son. Thank you."

"Have you talked to Sobrina?"

"I've tried to call Sobrina three times and even left a long message, told her that her boy is missing." Wilma sighed. "Your sister doesn't really want to talk with me right now. And besides, Lord knows where she is . . ."

Keith was overcome with heaviness. "We gotta find Malik, Ma." He spoke in barely a whisper. "After all our family has been through, he was the one that I knew was going to take the next big step. If he's gone on and done something stupid—something foolish—I don't know if I can—"

His mother stopped him. "You just need to keep praying. What else can we do in times like these? We need to be praying, son."

"Praying for what?" Keith muttered.

Wilma placed her chilled and aged hand around her coffee mug and gripped it tightly. "Praying that he'd come home—that wherever he is, and whatever he's done, God will just send our boy home." Her voice wavered as her words stuck in her throat. She dabbed quickly at a tear that nestled in one of the wrinkles around her eye.

Keith grabbed a picture frame on his desk and studied it for a moment. The image inside was three years old. In it Uncle Keith had his arms around Camron and Malik. All three of them were dressed in suits and ties. They had just finished hearing a well-known sociologist from Harvard speaking at a local fundraiser. Their expressions were serious, confident, and serene. They looked poised to wrestle with and triumph over their universe.

What had happened to the three men in that picture? Keith wondered. What had once looked certain was now fragmented. The phone trembled slightly in his hand.

22

THE SURRENDER

1:07 p.m., Tuesday before Thanksgiving

THE LONG GRAVEL ROAD WAS COMING TO AN END.
The sheriff continued to race behind the Lexus as they
drew closer to the county highway. Jim glanced at the
dash. The all-too-familiar gas light was on. He knew that
they wouldn't get much further before this escape came
to a grinding halt. He hoped that it would be the gas that
would stop them and not an icy crash.

Malik could no longer feel his face. He blinked
constantly in an attempt to keep the cold out of his eyes.

■ ■ ■

Sheriff Jefferson cursed as a hidden pothole jarred his
vehicle. Just then his radio came on. "Sheriff, this is
Dispatch . . . The Lexus belongs to a Jim Dawkins. A

report from the city verifies that the vehicle was seen in Edgewood last night. It's possible that Jim was carjacked and kidnapped. The black suspect is believed to be armed and dangerous. Over."

"What's this carjacking city thug doing all the way out here?" the sheriff mumbled to himself.

■ ■ ■

Jim leaned over as far as he could, put his hand on Malik's shoulder, and gave it a squeeze. "Slow down! Slow down! This gravel road is about to end! The highway is probably frozen over!"

Malik took his foot off the gas and pressed the brakes. The car ground to a sudden halt about ten feet from the edge of the highway. He paused for a moment and looked quickly to his left and to his right. To the right the road had several curves and turns. To the left the road was long and straight.

Jim's heart was racing. He fumbled with the seat belt to attempt an escape. But before he could do so, Malik revved the car into action again.

■ ■ ■

Sheriff Jefferson watched the Lexus turn onto the highway and then snatched his radio off his dash. "Suspect is heading west on County Road 63," he spoke gruffly. "I repeat: Suspect is heading west on County Road 63. Over."

Another voice crackled over the radio. "Sheriff, this

is Officers Smith and Lenoix. We're heading east on 63 now. We're two miles from your position. How should we proceed? Over."

The sheriff slowed his vehicle to a halt and then cautiously drove out onto the highway. "Set up a roadblock in one mile. I am still in pursuit."

■ ■ ■

Malik felt sick. He had run from gangbangers before. He had fled from two parties where gunshots were fired. There was the time he raced away from the police after he stole some candy from a convenience store. There was something dreadful and yet thrilling in each of those moments. But this present moment was filled with nothing but terror.

Jim was praying under his breath. He gripped the handle on the ceiling with white-knuckled hands. Cold clouds of breath emerged from his mouth as the icy air rushed into the car. He watched with fascination and horror as Malik navigated the treacherous road, his head still hanging out the window. They were going no more than forty miles an hour, but it felt like eighty. The car fishtailed, and Malik moved to the middle of the road to give himself as much room for error as possible. Jim spun around in his seat. Through the semi-frosted back window, he could see swirling blue lights in the distance.

Malik cursed angrily as he spotted the police car and orange cones in the distance. They had wedged themselves perfectly—he could not get around them without driving on the shoulder of the road.

■ ■ ■

"We got you now, boy!" Sheriff Jefferson said as he slapped his dash victoriously. "Hey—what in the world is he trying to do?" The Lexus had angled off toward the left. The sheriff stared in surprise as the Lexus attempted to straddle the shoulder and the road. "He isn't gonna try it, is he?"

■ ■ ■

Malik could feel and hear the car slipping. It was a miracle he had made it this far. The officers ahead were out of their vehicles and waving their arms for him to stop. Suddenly the car felt like it was lifted into the air. Malik could tell that he was no longer in control.

The Lexus went into a free skid on a patch of ice and slammed violently into a large tree. It spun ninety degrees before bouncing back out onto the road, just thirty yards from the blockade.

Malik's seat belt was unbuckled, and his face and torso collided viciously into the airbag. His head and neck were lashed backward. He heard the sound of crunching metal and broken glass.

Jim's face was thrown into the passenger side window with a thud. Syrupy, warm blood began to trickle from the gash on his face.

Together, Jim and Malik sat in the crashed car, stunned.

■ ■ ■

Sheriff Jefferson watched as plumes of steam rose out of the crumpled hood of the car. He carefully decelerated his vehicle on the precarious road and reached for his radio again.

"Suspect has crashed his vehicle. Requesting immediate medical assistance. Over."

He put his SUV in park, stepped out, and pulled his pistol from its holster. "Get out of the vehicle with your hands in the air!" he bellowed.

Officers Smith and Lenoix also removed their guns and trained them on the Lexus. The sheriff proceeded to holler instructions. Steam continued to rise from the Lexus. But there was no movement inside until, slowly, the front door opened. A young man stepped out in front of them.

■ ■ ■

Malik took a moment to look at all three officers. Their faces appeared angry, and the guns pointed in his direction looked decisive. He could see the sheriff shouting at him. His mouth opened and closed, but the words were dissonant, indecipherable to Malik's ears. Suddenly he heard Jim's voice and felt him tugging at his sweatshirt. He turned his head to look back inside the vehicle.

"Come on, Malik!" Jim pleaded. "Just do what they say! Get your hands in the air before they hurt you!"

Malik looked down at Jim and noticed the blood

streaming slowly from above his eye. He turned back to face
the police. It was up to him: His arms would initiate the
process of either surrender or suicide. He could reach for the
sky or for his gun.

Despite the overwhelming weight of despair, Malik did
not wish to die. So reluctantly and slowly, he raised his
hands above his head. A wave of regret passed over him,
followed quickly by a wave of relief.

"Now step away from the vehicle. Slowly . . . slowly . . ."
The sheriff was hollering directions to Malik, waving him to
the side with his gun.

Malik did as he was told and moved out from behind the
car door. He squinted in the midday sun.

"Get down on your knees!" the sheriff barked.

Jim remained in the vehicle, watching Malik, praying
that he would continue to cooperate. The young man
dropped to his knees, his hands still high in the air. As he
did so, the gun jostled loose from his waistband and fell to
the ground in front of him.

For a moment everyone looked at the gun. It lay there,
awkwardly and menacingly, settled in an inch of glistening powder. The police stiffened and leaned in with their
own pistols.

"He's got a gun!" Officer Smith yelled hoarsely.

"Listen!" Sheriff Jefferson shouted. "Slowly . . . slowly . . .
slide the gun away from you. Do it! Do it now!"

Malik looked down at the gun and then back at the police
with their guns trained on him. Each breath that he took felt

strained and required a concerted effort. He was nearly paralyzed with fear. He leaned forward to do as he was told.

"He's going for it!" Officer Smith cried out.

"Careful!" the sheriff instructed again through clenched
teeth. "Slide it slowly!"

Jim felt like a helpless spectator to this drama. He wanted
to do something—anything. Suddenly he burst forth from
the passenger door and stood to his feet.

Jim's abrupt decision startled the police. They turned their
attention toward him. Meanwhile, Malik had placed his hand
on top of the gun. His hands were so cold he could barely
even feel it at all. He flexed his arm slightly to shove it away
from him.

Two sharp shots rang out along the county highway.

■ ■ ■

Malik felt a fiery pain in his right shoulder. The pain in his
chest was different. He sensed breath and life itself seeping
from the hole the bullet had created. His body fell backward
onto the icy road.

"Shots fired! Shots fired!" Sheriff Jefferson shouted into
his radio. "Suspect down. I repeat: suspect down. We need
immediate medical attention."

Jim raced around the Lexus toward Malik, who lay on the
ground clutching his chest. Short, ragged breaths emerged
from his mouth. Officer Lenoix kicked the gun off to the
side and knelt down beside Malik. A dark pool of blood was
painting the snow beneath him.

"He was going for the gun!" Officer Smith said resolutely. He looked at the sheriff and his partner for confirmation. The sheriff glanced at Jim, but he just stood there wide-eyed, his hands on his head. From down the road they could hear the shrill wail of ambulance sirens.

23

THE BEGINNING

Eight hours later

JIM WINCED SLIGHTLY as he struggled to put on his coat. "Careful, honey," Mary Beth said softly as she tried to help him. "I don't understand why you won't just stay the night and come home in the morning. You need to rest." Her father sat in a chair in the corner with his arms folded stiffly across his chest.

"I'm fine," Jim said, and he offered a reassuring smile. "Stitches and a mild concussion are not enough for me to want to spend the night in a country-hospital bed. No thanks!"

"It's more than that. You've been kidnapped at gunpoint. Held hostage. Nearly frozen to death. And then a terrible car accident. You need your rest, honey." She gave him a long hug and nestled her face in his chest. Grateful tears emerged in her eyes and rolled slowly down her cheeks. She hadn't stopped hugging him since she had arrived at the hospital three hours ago.

Jim pulled her close. It felt nice to have her warm body in his arms.

Just then there was a knock at the door. The three of them turned. "I'm sorry to interrupt." Detective MarQuan Cole introduced himself to Jim and nodded to Mary Beth and her father. "Mrs. Dawkins . . . Congressman . . . It's good to see you again—this time under better circumstances." He turned again to Jim. "I'm glad to see that you're up on your feet, Mr. Dawkins."

"Yeah, I feel fine," Jim said. "I'm thankful."

"I'm going to need to ask you a few questions," Detective Cole said.

"Now?" Mary Beth asked. She cocked her head to the side and raised her eyebrows. "Couldn't that wait a while?"

"I'm afraid not," the detective replied, shaking his head. "An awful lot has happened over the last twenty-four hours or so. There are a lot of different details swirling in the wind right now, and a young man's life hangs in the balance in more ways than one. We need to get this information together while it's fresh. We—"

Mary Beth's face soured. "Excuse me! That young man put my husband's life in danger. Whose side are you on here? That boy—"

"That boy," Congressman Lawrey roared as he stood up from his chair, "should be in jail! He's lucky just to be alive after all of the ridiculous and asinine things he's done. He's the one you should be interrogating!"

"I intend to talk to him, sir," Detective Cole said calmly. "But the young man is unconscious right now."

The old man's face was red and twitching. "He nearly killed Jim in five different ways. My daughter and my wife haven't slept in over twenty-four hours because of him! My wife is so weak and ill from all of this nonsense that she couldn't even make the trip here to the hospital. Jim is battered. He's bleeding. He's tired. Hasn't he been through enough? Haven't all of us been through enough? Do you really want to add to all of our pain right now?"

Detective Cole raised his hand. "I know your family has been through a tremendous ordeal. And I don't want to pile on more, but I'm just doing my job. Mr. Dawkins, your testimony is very important. I can't overstate that."

"This is unbelievable!" Mary Beth said, her nostrils flaring. Jim grabbed her hand and gave it a slight squeeze. She shot him an angry glance and locked her jaw.

The detective continued. "We need to make certain we know what happened last night—all of it." He held out his hand. "Mr. Dawkins, why don't you take a seat?"

Jim glanced at his wife and then at the detective, then sat down on the edge of the hospital bed. Mary Beth frowned and sat down beside him. The congressman just stood there, glowering. Detective Cole pulled out his notepad and removed the pen from behind his ear. He offered up a smile.

"So, let's start from the beginning. What happened at that gas station last night?"

■ ■ ■

Wilma dabbed her eyes with the shredded piece of tissue balled in her tiny fist. She sat beside Malik's hospital bed, his hand in her own. His eyes were closed, and his face betrayed a weakened agony. A tube was in his mouth, and various wires were fixed to his body.

A colleague from the college had brought Keith to the hospital. He sat in his wheelchair at the foot of the bed, staring at his nephew. LeKeisha was leaning against the wall, stirring a straw in a foam cup of coffee. Malik's mother, Sobrina, was slumped in a seat with her head in her hands. Her eyes were bloodshot as she stared blankly out of the window. Aside from some chatter in the hallway, the only sound in the room was the dull chirp of the bedside monitor.

A short, fat doctor entered the room, holding some paperwork in his hands. A large red nose, propping up a pair of thick black glasses, dominated his face. With his eyes fixed on his charts, he started speaking to no one in particular. "Hello everyone. I'm Dr. Patterson. So, our friend Malik is in pretty bad shape, but he was lucky. The bullet grazed one of his lungs, ricocheted off his ribs and narrowly missed his heart. We aren't out of the woods just yet though. He's lost a ton of blood. We were able to remove the bullet from his shoulder, and we'll try to fish out the other one once his condition stabilizes."

"When will he be conscious?" Uncle Keith asked tersely.

The doctor looked up from his chart and offered Keith a slight shrug. "It could be soon . . . or it might be a while. He's weak and exhausted—"

"I'm looking forward to asking my nephew how and why those bullets ended up inside of him in the first place," Keith replied.

Dr. Patterson awkwardly cleared his throat but said nothing.

"That question can wait a minute, Keith," Wilma chided her scowling son.

"Why is *he* here?" Sobrina asked icily. She pointed to an armed white officer standing just outside the doorway, his back to the room.

The doctor blushed slightly before he spoke. "He's here for everyone's protection."

"Whose protection?" Keith snapped. "Ours? Yours? Malik's? Whose?"

"Look," the doctor stammered. "We'll be monitoring Malik's situation very closely and give you some updates as we get them. In the meantime, you're welcome to stay here with him. It would be good for him to see loved ones when he wakes up." The doctor moved quickly to the door as he spoke.

Once the family was alone again, Keith cracked his knuckles and shook his head. "This is absurd. They've got an armed guard posted outside the room like Malik is some kind of terrorist. Unbelievable!"

"They're the ones who tried to kill my baby," Sobrina snarled.

"Everyone needs to hush." Wilma's voice was trembling. "All of that can come later. Right now we need to pray that Malik will just open his eyes. He's all that matters right now. He's the reason we're all here. Let's just focus our attention on our sweet boy."

· · ·

"Well," Detective Cole said, closing his notebook. He had taken nearly three pages of notes. "I think that's all of my questions for now. Is there anything else you want to add to your statements?"

Jim looked at his wife for a moment and then shook his head. "No. I think that's about it."

The detective pursed his lips and nodded slightly. "Okay then." He tucked his pen behind his ear. "Thank you for your time. If I need anything else, I'll be in touch."

"Any word on Malik?" Jim asked.

"I'm on my way to see him now," the detective responded. "I heard they moved him from the trauma unit to a room about thirty minutes ago."

"I think I'd like to see him too."

"Come on, Jim," Mary Beth said, trying to reason with him. "Tonight? Now? Let's just get you home—please."

Jim placed his hand on her shoulder. "We'll go home shortly, honey. I want to see him."

The detective nodded as he headed toward the door. "Then you can follow me."

Mary Beth looked hopefully to her father. "You coming, Daddy?"

The congressman waved his hands in disgust. "You go on without me. I have no desire to see that boy. I'll meet you in the lobby."

Detective Cole led Jim and Mary Beth to the elevator. They rode in silence to the second floor. From there the detective led the way to Malik's room. His cell phone rang, and he glanced at it for a moment before answering the call. "Hello?" He held the phone to his ear. "Really? . . . Is he able to speak? . . . Okay. Okay. I'm heading that way. I'll be there shortly." He turned to face Jim and his wife. "I'm afraid I need to run. The store owner from the gas station has regained consciousness." He walked backward toward the elevator. "I need to speak with him. Malik's room is right around the corner. Room 297." With that, the detective turned and left.

Jim and Mary Beth stood for a moment before Mary Beth broke the silence. "Jim, why do you want to see this kid right now—after all that's happened between you and him?" She shook her head. "I don't feel comfortable with this at all."

Jim sighed. "I don't really know. I just want to see if he's all right, I guess. Come on. I won't stay long. I promise."

Together they continued down the hall toward Room 297.

An armed guard was posted at the door. They could hear voices inside. "Is this Malik Thompson's room?" Jim asked.

The guard nodded.

"May I see him for a moment?"

The guard studied Jim's bruised face and his stitches for a moment. "And you are?"

"I'm Jim Dawkins. I was with him through most of this . . . ordeal . . . I'd just like to see him for a second, if that's okay."

The guard turned and let Jim and Mary Beth pass. Jim drew a deep breath and took one step inside. He spotted Malik's battered frame attached to the wires and the machines. He noticed Wilma sitting beside him, cupping his hand to her face. There was Uncle Keith in the wheelchair. He guessed that the other two women were his aunt and his mother. In an odd way he felt as though he knew each of them.

They were staring at him. He could see in their eyes a wide-ranging jury of emotions. Anger. Curiosity. Contempt. Pain. He wanted to say something, but the ability to speak betrayed him.

Mary Beth stood in the doorway, fidgeting with her gold necklace. She was unwilling to enter, but now that they had all seen her, she was unable to leave.

Wilma mustered a warm smile and spoke softly. "Hello, Jim."

He slowly raised his hand and attempted a smile of his own.

As soon as Wilma spoke Jim's name, everyone in the room knew who he was. In a small space where almost everyone felt like a victim, silence ruled the room.

Jim and the family maintained their weighty stillness for nearly a minute. Jim felt a bit as if he were on trial. He dropped his eyes to the floor.

Just then Wilma felt the hand in her own begin to stir. She gasped, ever so slightly, as she watched Malik's wearied and weakened eyes flutter and struggle to open. All eyes turned to his bed. He was awake; he appeared to be alert. Smiles erupted on all of their faces as they pressed in around him.

Malik exchanged a brief glance with everyone in his family, but Wilma noticed that he kept returning his gaze to the doorway. She looked up in that direction. Her grandson's eyes were locked with Jim's.

Mary Beth grabbed her husband's hand and gently tried to pull him away. But he would not budge. He and Malik beheld one another in solemn silence.

The distance between them was little more than a leap.

AFTERWORD

ON JULY 12, 2013, in the middle of a segregated city, our church seemed a model multicultural gathering. Our small-group meetings were diverse. Our pastoral staff was diverse. The music performed on Sunday morning had no allegiance to a specific genre. It was the utopia of diversity that so many pastors desire today.

However, July 13, 2013, created a pivotal change at my church. That day, six Florida jurors acquitted George Zimmerman in the killing of teenager Trayvon Martin. Social media was ablaze with both adulation and condemnation.

July 14 was not a regular Sunday for many. Droves of Americans entered their churches with a heavy burden: the knowledge that they lived in a country that condoned injustice. Many sat waiting for the pastor to reconcile their concerns to a good and faithful God. However, many church services went on as though the world outside wasn't experiencing a traumatic event. There was no mention of the case. There was no attempt to touch the tension.

I have to admit that I was livid. I did not expect my pastors to approach the stage wearing hoodies in veneration of Trayvon. However, I did expect them to pause from their regularly scheduled agenda to address a pronounced tension in our congregation. Many of the minority members of the church felt there was an elephant that needed to be addressed, a national issue that carried heavy implications regarding their identity. Many of the white members wondered why this was such a big deal to people who had no relational connection to Trayvon. The division was obvious—and yet disregarded. For months there was only silent hope that this agitation would go away. It never did.

What did we need in that moment? We needed reconciliation. We needed to talk!

I would reason that my church is a microcosm of America. Brothers and sisters, we need to talk! Furthermore, when we talk we need to not assume the worst in each other but affirm the image of God in one another. This is precisely what *Meals from Mars* is attempting to do.

Conversations around race can be toxic, difficult, and subversive. However, one of the most destructive ways to enter into a conversation about race is to ignore that we have different opinions and experiences. What I learned about our church community is that we shared in proximity but lacked in authenticity. We sacrificed crucial conversations for the sake of apparent harmony. That is not love, nor does it produce true community.

To live as if we are all the same is to be foolish and irre-
sponsible. We acknowledge variety in the animal kingdom.
A zebra is beautiful because of its design. It's admired
because it's different from the stallion. We appreciate the
variations of the seasons in a year. We don't ignore the snow
when it falls. Many in the faith community are well-meaning
people who desire unity across racial and cultural lines.
Therefore they declare they are "colorblind." However, the
declaration of colorblindness doesn't remove the tension. It
perpetuates a dangerous narrative that how God created me
isn't fascinating enough to acknowledge. The simplest indi-
cation of ethnic importance is the fact that God made us this
way. All his creation was good!

When we *do* decide to talk, we cannot sweep the truth of
history under the rug of reconciliation. We must deal with
truth in order to get to reconciliation. We must approach the
table with our feelings and agendas submitted to the glorious
Lord, speaking candidly from our personal experience.

We must also be allowed to mess up without the threat
of being labeled racists or race baiters. We must approach
these conversations with reckless compassion—the kind of
compassion that may be misunderstood and mistreated but
that still extends a hand of grace.

I ask that we stop ignoring racial differences and love
each other *in light of* our differences. We should desire to
know and understand our brothers and sisters so we can love
them and God better. Our color matters because our iden-
tities matter. We are creations of the Most High—a motley

demonstration of his creativity. He desires that we find every aspect of our differences in the intentional design of creation.

Outside the gospel, there is every reason to hoard power and privilege. But in the house of God we are called to consider others before ourselves. Outside the gospel, there is legitimacy in feeling bitter when offended. But in the house of God, it brings dignity to turn the other cheek.

I would commission us all to be slow to speak and quick to listen, to surrender our presuppositions so that true dialogue can take place. We must throw away bitterness and entitlement because we are indebted to the Maker of all creation, and we must be ready to forgive as Christ forgave us. I believe *Meals from Mars* can push us in the direction that creates authentic dialogue.

In August 2014, an unarmed teenager, Michael Brown, was shot and killed by a police officer in Ferguson, Missouri. Once again we had a traumatic event in our country. However, there was a different response from my church. Our pastors tackled the issue head-on. We had church-led discussions around race and culture. People were able to vent, cry, and argue about the state of America. Once emotions were released, we felt one step closer to real community and reconciliation. I praise God for the courage and wisdom displayed in our leaders. It's time for that same courage and wisdom to be displayed throughout America.

Now let's talk!!

SHO BARAKA

FOR DISCUSSION

Meals from Mars is a complicated story, touching on tender issues of race, class, privilege, personal pain, and systemic cultural challenges. Please use the following questions to guide your conversation about these difficult issues.

1. The novel opens in the middle of the story, with Malik and Jim crashed at the side of the road, surrounded by police. What was your first impression of Jim? Of Malik?

2. Jim and Mary Beth are very generous in buying groceries for Malik's family. But they're not enthusiastic about this act of kindness. Can you identify with their frustration at the beginning of the story? Why or why not?

3. Jim is proud that his church provides groceries for Malik's family. But Malik challenges him on it. Who's right, do you think? Why?

4. Malik is particularly annoyed by two things associated with the groceries from Mars Chapel: selfies and hummus. Why was he so put off by those things? What might the church have done differently?
5. What responsibility, if any, does Mars Chapel (Jim's church) have to provide for the family of Wilma Thompson (Malik's grandmother)? Was the church living up to its responsibility? Why or why not?
6. What should Malik have done when he felt threatened at the convenience store? What would you have done?
7. What should Jim have done when Malik jumped in his car? What would you have done?
8. Do you know of anyone who's had an experience like Uncle Keith's, when he was pulled over by the police? How was that person affected by the experience?
9. Do you know of anyone who's had an experience like Jim's friend Sam, when he was mugged while fixing power lines in Edgewood? How was that person affected by the experience?
10. Think about your own community. Where do you observe racial divides like the ones between Edgewood and Stone Brook? What perpetuates the divide? What could be done to heal whatever racial divide exists?
11. What needs to happen first? Why?
12. Malik argues that much of Jim's success in life has something to do with an inherent *privilege*—the system was set up to support Jim, even as it was

rigged against Malik. Does Malik's argument ring true for you? Why or why not?

13. Jim argues that "choices have consequences"—that most people's troubles are the result of their own bad decisions. Does his argument ring true for you? Why or why not?

14. Whom did you tend to find yourself agreeing with more—Jim or Malik? Why?

15. Whom did you identify with more—Wilma (Malik's grandmother) or Keith (Malik's uncle)? Why?

16. What did you hear from Malik or Jim that was most uncomfortable for you? What made it uncomfortable?

17. Mars Chapel looms in the background of *Meals from Mars*, and throughout the story there are little allusions to prayer. Where is God in this story? What role does faith have to play in difficult social issues like those in *Meals from Mars*?

18. The novel opens with Malik and Jim surrounded by police. Were you surprised by how that scene was resolved toward the end of the novel? Why or why not?

19. What do you think Jim was thinking as he stared at Malik in his hospital room at the end of the novel? What do you think Malik was thinking?

20. Imagine an ending for this story. What happens to Malik? To Jim? What happens to their relationship? Why do you think that's how the story ends?

ADDITIONAL RESOURCES

The following are helpful resources as you continue to explore issues of racial justice and reconciliation.

BOOKS
Ta-Nehisi Coates, *Between the World and Me*
Christena Cleveland, *Disunity in Christ*
Michael Emerson and Christian Smith, *Divided by Faith*
Carl Ellis, *Free at Last?*
Timothy Keller, *Generous Justice*
Frederick Douglass, *Narrative of the Life of Frederick Douglass*
Michelle Alexander, *The New Jim Crow*
W. E. B. Du Bois, *The Souls of Black Folk*
Benjamin Watson, *Under Our Skin*

ALBUMS
Lecrae, *Anomaly*
Jackie Hill Perry, *The Art of Joy*
Dre Murray and Alex Faith, *Southern Lights: Overexposed*
Sho Baraka, *Talented Xth* and *The Narrative*

ACKNOWLEDGMENTS

This book wouldn't have been possible without the contributions of some special people.

Sho, thank you for editing and critiquing the initial manuscript. Thank you also for all your contributions to my last two books. Your friendship has been a gift, and your music has shaped a lot of my thinking.

Thanks to Don and David at NavPress. I'm grateful for your willingness to take a chance on me and this book.

Jason, God has used you in more ways than you know to keep me encouraged and keep me going. Our conversations over coffee have been crucial. I think it's your turn to buy.

Matt, thanks for always being there for me over the years. You've seen me at my highest and my lowest and have always been there to cheer me on or pick me up.

Brian—wow! We've been challenging each other and trying to tackle life together for more than twenty years. You've pushed me to be better in almost every way possible, and your friendship is something I genuinely cherish.

Sam and Ty, I'm blessed to have brothers like you. You both in different ways have kept my ship afloat. I appreciate you.

I want to thank everyone involved with Restoration Academy. Without RA this book would never have existed.

Mom and Dad, thanks for praying for me, and thank you for putting a pen in my hands a long time ago and telling me to write.

Sara, the fact that you loved this story first fueled me to finish.

Doc Gordon, thanks for mentoring me and always being available. Your wisdom and love are invaluable.

Ron Carter, thanks for taking a chance on a naive twenty-two-year-old more than sixteen years ago, and for giving me a job at RA. And thanks for following up with me and encouraging me during my toughest season in ministry.

Adam Thomason, I appreciate you and our conversations. You continue to push me out of my comfort zones and challenge my paradigms. And that's a blessing.

Jesus, thank you for being my *shalom*. I pray that you use this meager effort to make *shalom*.

To everyone I've forgotten, please forgive me.

ABOUT THE AUTHOR

BEN SCIACCA currently serves as the executive director of Restoration Academy in Fairfield, Alabama. Ben has been involved at Restoration for sixteen years and has been invested in city ministry for more than twenty. He received his BA in history from Wheaton College and his master's in educational leadership from Covenant College. He is the author of *Kai'Ro: The Journey of an Urban Pilgrim*, *Kai'Ro Returns*, and *Urban Shepherds*. Ben speaks at national conferences and provides consultation regarding urban education. He enjoys soccer, football, and disc golf. He, his wife Sara, and their four children live in the neighborhood where he serves.

TWITTER: @IAMJUDAHBEN

RESTORATION ACADEMY is a private, urban, and Christ-centered school in Fairfield, Alabama. For the last twenty-seven years, Restoration has been seeking to provide a high-quality and Christ-centered education to inner-city youth in the Birmingham area. The school currently serves close to three hundred students in kindergarten through twelfth grade. Restoration exists to provide a safe and nurturing education where youth can thrive. For the last ten years, 100 percent of Restoration's seniors have been admitted to college. The hope is that these incredible students will graduate with the skills, character, and vision to be agents of change in the world around them.

LEARN MORE ABOUT RESTORATION ACADEMY AT HTTP://WWW.RESTORATIONACADEMY.ORG.